CATECHISM
WITH THOUGHTS FROM THE CURÉ OF ARS

CATECHISM

with thoughts from the Curé of Ars
(St John Vianney)

Translated from the French
of Hugues d'Orfeuille
by
Alan Bancroft

ST PAULS

Original title: *Catéchisme avec pensées du curé d'Ars*
French copyright © Pierre Téqui éditeur, 82 rue Bonaparte, 75006 Paris, France.
Cover design: Manoj Pal

Nihil obstat:
Father Ian Farrell
7 March 2011

Imprimatur:
Father Anthony Kay, Vicar General
Diocese of Salford,
8 March 2011

ST PAULS Publishing
187 Battersea Bridge Road, London SW11 3AS, UK
www.stpaulspublishing.com

ISBN 978-0-85439-805-8

A catalogue record is available for this book from the British Library.

Set by Tukan DTP, Stubbington, Fareham, UK
Printed by Melita Press, Paola, Malta

ST PAULS is an activity of the priests and brothers of the Society of St Paul who proclaim the Gospel through the media of social communication.

Jesus replied:
"My teaching does not come from me [alone],
but from Him who sent me [the Father]."

John 7:16

When the poor Pope, when the bishops and the priests
teach doctrine, they are but the servants of Christ.
That doctrine does not come from us:
it is the doctrine of Christ;
we ought simply to guard it and make it known."

Pope John Paul I
Audience on 13 September 1978

Contents

BOOK TWO: Grace and the Sacraments

BOOK THREE: The Moral Law. The Commandments

PREFACE

by
Rt. Rev. Patrick O'Donoghue
Bishop Emeritus, Lancaster

Question: *What is a catechism?*
Answer: *A catechism is a summary of the main teachings about religion in the form of questions and answers.*

That sounds very dry, but in fact a good catechism will fill us with wonder and enthusiasm for our faith and help us to hear the whole "symphony of faith" in its simplicity and glory. It shows us the truth, beauty and goodness of God's words and deeds.

Every Catholic has a duty to assist in passing on to others the Faith handed down from the Apostles. A catechism is an essential tool for use in this work.

Jesus commissioned the Church to "go ... and make disciples of all nations, baptizing them ... and teaching them..." (Matthew 28:19-20). Catechisms have been developed to help the Church fulfil this commission, especially in preparing people for baptism and the other sacraments.

Although the Trinity of Father, Son and Holy Spirit encompasses many mysteries too great for us to know, catechisms help us to understand more about the revealed Faith and to communicate it to others in a simple and direct manner. At the same time we are ourselves able to enter more deeply into these sacred mysteries.

Catechisms help us to know more about our Faith and the historical Church's knowledge and understanding of God. But, even more important, they help us come closer to the *love* of a living person – Jesus Christ. When you fall in love you want to know everything about the one you love. That is what catechisms do, they help us to fall deeper in love with God.

This catechism sets out the truths of our Catholic Faith in a simple and accessible way and links its teaching with thoughts from that simple and saintly teacher of the Faith, St John Vianney. I recommend this book to all – to those taking the early steps towards learning about the Church and the Catholic Faith, to those teaching others, and to anyone who wants to become better equipped to do the Lord's command.

AUTHOR'S NOTE

Having learned (and then taught) an excellent little catechism in my diocese of Nantes, I am anxious to pass on to children the elements of a serious theology. I am proud of getting back to the thought of the great philosopher Étienne Gilson when he declared that children should be given solid food: and that the teaching of the catechism is the most important food a Christian can receive. And then Étienne Gilson added that such teaching should be the immediate bearer of all the truth it can contain.[1]

Let me give some precise details of this textbook. First – the **WORDS TO READ** set forth the subject of the lesson in 'condensed' terms: which it is for all to complete, through their religious culture or from written sources. Second – the **QUESTIONS AND ANSWERS TO LEARN**. These should first of all be clearly explained. St Augustine said: "There is no better way of seeking truth than to proceed by questions and answers."[2] All these questions and answers, of course, are for learning 'by heart', to be recited. This is essential if one wants children to keep hold of clear and precise notions on the doctrinal plan, and to be preserved from heresy. Third – the **WORDS TO THINK ABOUT** are chosen from among the writings of St John Vianney, the holy Curé of Ars. It is good to make children savour the beauty of each saying. In that way they will pick up the habit of meditating.

Hugues d'Orfeuille

---

1. E. Gilson, Le philosophe et la théologie, pp. 74-75.
2. St Augustine, *Soliloques*, II. VII, 14.

INTRODUCTION

by
Dr. Ernest Huant
(1909–1993)
sometime President of the *Societé philosophique des Sciences* and of the *Centre international Humanae Vitae*

A small work, this; but the slimness of the volume ought not to lead to any illusion of diminished importance. For in fact it is a very deep volume, the echoes of which in souls can only be deeper still – especially when it's a question of the young souls of children, for whom above all the author intends it.

It is, then, a catechism that M. Hugues d'Orfeuille offers us. But what strikes one on reading this work is that the words we find in it are precise and doctrinal. We are a long way from the triviality, the insipidity, of those pale substitutes found in so many publications – childish rather than childlike – emanating from those who still have the temerity to misrepresent the true intentions of the Second Vatican Council.

And it is a very happy touch that the author has drawn attention, by his quotation from St John's Gospel (7:16) and the words of Pope John Paul I (at the audience at Rome on 13 September 1978) to what is the keystone of his whole construction – *Doctrine, not from men but from Christ, and therefore from God!*

That is what he intends to affirm, and to comment upon, to children. That, too, is the starting-point from which he will strive to draw forth the moral law and its Commandments, always at the level of the same young readers. Thus, the very construction of this one work stands out as threefold – a Trinitarian sign in which it pleases one to see a happy token of success!

The truths to believe unfold in accordance with the articles of the Creed and through a method of presentation (which will be continued throughout) comprising Words to read, and then Questions and answers to learn!... Yes, dear reader, you haven't misread that – "to *learn*"! What a pleasure it is to find this master-word which has governed all human understanding, and which so many today with inadequate understanding of its value would like to outlaw, especially for the child – the child who (isn't it so?) is not of an age to understand or choose – and which they would like to replace by the vapidity of comparisons more or less skilfully suggested or uttered. *Learn!* No, Christ isn't just "one of your buddies"; He is God, Son of God.

This very simple Catechism of M. d'Orfeuille's, then, is not timid in giving things their name. It knows no dread of words. What a relief to adult believers – even those who have reached the very heights of "intellectualism" (or so they think) – from finding here, in the domain of the sacred, words that have no fear of themselves. And let us be very certain that children, eager for certitude above everything, won't for their part have a fear of those same words!

I'm pleased to call attention to the fact that sometimes this little volume contains precise details that I for one don't remember seeing in former catechisms, but which have fully satisfied my own mind. For example, its rightly noting that it was as man, and not as God, that Christ was born, suffered, died, rose from the dead, ascended to heaven;[1] and also that after His death on the cross the Divinity of Jesus will remain united eternally to His soul and *to His body!* Through well learning and understanding such things, children will in later years be ready with very solid arguments in reply to unbelievers (from various circles) whom they may meet and talk with.

The safeguarding of the spiritual life – that is to say, the explanations of grace and sin with which the author arrives at the *second book* in this catechism – opens up for the child a domain that is particularly complex. In general, children either go through printed words falteringly, or at first attempt 'erase' them from their minds, or, sometimes, trip and fall into the terrible trap of scruples. Here, I have found M. d'Orfeuille's words, and his questions and answers, particularly valuable in their living simplicity. Here, too, there is no doctoring of anything, no deliberate omissions! Original sin is not avoided. The Eucharist is clearly defined and developed, in a series of *ascending questions and answers* which are perfectly adapted to the mind of a child, and which from that point of view seem to me to be a real little marvel of precision and opening of the topic at the same time. So it is, also, with the role of the Mass. *Children fundamentally want to go all the way through a subject.* They will very well understand that the Mass is a making-present again of the Sacrifice of the Cross; but they will remain unsatisfied, hungry, if

---

1. Though the One who was thus born, suffered, died, rose from the dead, ascended, was Himself the Divine Person of the Word, God the Son: see page 47, questions and answers 5 and 6 (translator).

they are not taught – as catechists do often omit to teach them – what the Mass can do *for themselves and their fellow young people,* namely grant them graces won by Christ's Sacrifice.

The moral law, in an exposition of the Commandments, is the subject of the *third book* of this catechism, and the author seems to me to have been particularly inspired in making this a way of crowning the work. Here again, there is *no concession, no omission,* and *no timidity* either. The case of employers and workers is well mentioned, as is appropriate, in relation to the Fourth Commandment, with the *obligation of reciprocity* that both have. And, reciprocally also, the duties of Church and Country *towards us,* with the limits of obedience.

Those allusions (made by discreet touches, but very precise as well) to problems which unhappily form a sinister backcloth to our age – like abortion, like murder for "ridding us" of the malformed, of incurables and of old people who are "too ill" – come and give here an assurance that *this catechism forgets nothing!* Nothing that can *already structure* the mind of young children and thus *already protect* them against the future garbage of insanities of every kind that won't be lacking, alas! Protecting them from being perverted, in ear and mind, in the course of their next stages of growth. Future "sex education" might come, and all its sequels of brutalising deviations, but this catechism will have been able to teach the child, quite tranquilly, without cover-up or hypocrisy, that the Ninth Commandment forbids a man to desire someone else's wife, and also forbids one to accept and take pleasure in all the impure thoughts this sin brings – adding, just as simply, that it's the same for a woman in regard to men. And adding further that the Seventh Commandment and its "You shall not steal" prohibits also fraud and *illicitly high profits!* How beneficially, but with what clear simplicity, all this is formulated! No need to appeal to the inroads of the subconscious or to the impact of heredity. I repeat: all this can, or will be able to come afterwards, in order to try and test various relating hypotheses. All that can come. With this catechism, for the child, for his or her mind, the avenues of the faith are already marked out. The guard-rails will also have been put in place!

In short, is it not the great merit of this catechism – and also a guarantee of its very probable efficacy – that it *places trust in the child* by having a pre-sentiment, *even now,* of the grown-up it is destined to become?

BOOK ONE

OUR CREDO:
TRUTHS TO BELIEVE

LESSON 1 – GOD

WORDS TO READ

**He who made the world,
He who sent us into this world, is *God!***

*God has existed always: He is Eternal
God is Almighty
God is present everywhere
God knows everything
God loves us: He is LOVE.*

When we came into the world, we did not yet know our Mums.

Well, our Mums loved us, they waited to see our first smile. By that smile, we responded to our Mum's love – we loved her in return!

In a similar way, He who sent us into the world, God who is so good, loved us first; and now we must love Him in return.

QUESTIONS AND ANSWERS TO LEARN

1. What is God?
God is a pure spirit, the Creator of Heaven and Earth, the Almighty, and the Sovereign Lord of all things.

2. Why cannot there be more than one "God"?
There cannot be more than one "God", for then none of them would be infinitely perfect, and therefore none of them would be "God".

3. Has God existed always?

Yes, God has existed always: He has never had a beginning, and will never have an end. He is Eternal.

4. Where is God?

God is everywhere.

5. If God is everywhere, why do we not see Him?

We do not see God because He is a pure spirit, and our eyes cannot see spirits because they have no bodies.

6. Does God see us?

Yes, God sees everything, He hears everything, He knows everything – even the most secret thoughts of our hearts.

7. Does God love us?

Yes, God loves us: He is Love, and we ought to love Him more than all else.

WORDS TO THINK ABOUT

"The one true happiness we can have on earth is to love God and to know that God loves us."

St John Vianney, Curé of Ars

LESSON 2 – THE MYSTERY OF THE HOLY TRINITY

WORDS TO READ

God makes Himself known to us through Mysteries.

We cannot understand a "Mystery", for it is beyond what our minds can grasp.

The greatest Mystery, that of the Holy Trinity, reveals to us that in God there are Three equal and distinct Persons:

- **The Father, Creator of Heaven and Earth,**
- **The Son, begotten of the Father from all eternity,**
- **The Holy Spirit, who in a mysterious way is the Love of the Father for the Son, and of the Son for the Father.**

One... in Three? *How might we represent that?*
Perhaps by a diagram? Let us take an equilateral triangle (equal sides and equal angles):

- The angle A represents the Father,
- The angle B represents the Son,
- The angle C represents the Holy Spirit.

And the surface represents the Divinity that belongs to the three!

All three are but ONE single triangle.

Thus, the three Persons are but one single and the same God, for they have but one single and the same Divinity, one single and the same substance.

QUESTIONS AND ANSWERS TO LEARN

1. Can we know God?

Yes, we can know God, but He is a hidden God, He reveals Himself to us through Mysteries.

2. What is a Mystery?

A Mystery is a Truth that we ought to believe, but that we cannot fully understand because it goes beyond what our minds can grasp.

3. What is the greatest Mystery in God?

The greatest Mystery in God is the Mystery of the Holy Trinity.

4. What is the Mystery of the Holy Trinity?

The Mystery of the Holy Trinity is the Mystery of One single God in Three equal and distinct Persons.

5. Who are the Three Persons of the Holy Trinity?

The Three Persons of the Holy Trinity are the Father, the Son and the Holy Spirit.

6. Is the Father God?

Yes, the Father is God.

7. Is the Son God?

Yes, the Son is God.

8. Is the Holy Spirit God?

Yes, the Holy Spirit is God.

9. Are there therefore three "Gods"?

No, these Three Persons are but One and the same God.

10. Why are these Three Persons but One and the same God?

These Three Persons are but One and the same God because they have but one and the same substance and one and the same Divinity.

WORDS TO THINK ABOUT

"Oh, how beautiful it is, dear children!
The Father is our Creator, the Son is our
Redeemer, and the Holy Spirit is our Guide."

St John Vianney

LESSON 3 – THE CREATION AND THE ANGELS

WORDS TO READ

In His love, God created the whole world,
the sun, the moon, the stars and our earth!

He created the oceans, the continents
He created the trees and the plants
He created the birds and the fish
He created all the animals.
Finally, He created man!

God is the Master of Life! But before creating man, God created spirits; these are the angels.

Now, among the angels a certain number revolted against God; these are the devils.

The angels seek to guide us towards God; we each have a guardian angel.

The devils seek to harm us and to separate us from God.

QUESTIONS AND ANSWERS TO LEARN

1. Has the world always existed?

No, the world has not always existed.

2. Who made the world?

God made the world.

3. How did God make the world?

God made the world from nothing: that is Creation.

4. Who governs the world?

God governs the world.

5. Who are the angels?

The angels are pure spirits whom God created to serve Him.

6. Who are the devils?

The devils are the angels who revolted against God.

WORDS TO THINK ABOUT

"Goodnight, my Guardian Angel, thank you for having guarded me all through today. Offer to God every beat of my heart while I sleep."

St John Vianney

LESSON 4 – THE CREATION OF MAN

WORDS TO READ

To complete His creation, God created a being lower than the angels but higher than the animals: *this is man.*

He gave him a body like the animals, but much more perfect, much more beautiful.

God, who is Spirit, and who created spirits (the angels), put into man a spirit, *a soul!*

God placed man upon earth, while at the same time elevating him to a higher order, which we call supernatural (meaning above the simply natural).

The first man was Adam, and the woman that God gave him, to keep him company, was Eve.

These are our first parents, because God granted them to produce other human beings.

QUESTIONS AND ANSWERS TO LEARN

1. Who created us and sent us into the world?
God created us and sent us into the world.

2. Why did God create us and send us into the world?
God created us and sent us into the world to know Him, love Him and serve Him; and, by those means, to obtain Life Eternal.

3. What is the name of the first man God created?
The first man is called Adam.

4. How did God create the first man?

God fashioned the body of the first man and gave him a spiritual soul.

5. What is a spiritual soul?

A spiritual soul is a spirit that God created from nothing.

6. Where did God place man?

God placed man in an earthly Paradise, where he was to be happy, filled with all the gifts of nature and of grace.

7. What is the name of the first woman?

The first woman is called Eve.

8. Why do we call Adam and Eve our first parents?

We call Adam and Eve our first parents because we are all descended from that first man and that first woman.

WORDS TO THINK ABOUT

"God has made each of us a combination of body and soul."

St John Vianney

LESSON 5 – ORIGINAL SIN. INCARNATION AND REDEMPTION

WORDS TO READ

Adam and Eve were created free, and in a state of innocence. Nevertheless they were *created* beings, and therefore subject to God, and they had to obey Him.

The devil, jealous of man, sought to turn him away from God, to make him disobey: that is temptation.

Adam and Eve listened to the devil and lost their happiness. That is *original sin,* an act of pride by which Adam and Eve forsook God, in order to pursue an untruth of the devil: "By disobeying God, you will be like gods."

In His goodness, God promised man to save him from sin. The Son of God was to make Himself man *(Incarnation)* and to undergo death on a cross in order to redeem us *(Redemption).*

QUESTIONS AND ANSWERS TO LEARN

1. In what state were Adam and Eve created?

Adam and Eve were created in a state of innocence.

2. Did Adam and Eve always remain in a state of innocence?

No, Adam and Eve lost their state of innocence. Urged by the devil, they sinned against God by tasting the fruit forbidden to them.[1]

---

1. Genesis "uses figurative language" to describe this event at the beginning of man's history: CCC, para. 390 (translator).

3. What are the consequences of that sin of our first parents?

The consequences of that sin are death, slavery to the devil, inclination towards evil, and all the miseries of our present life.

4. Are all human beings entangled in that sin and its consequences?

Yes, all human beings are entangled in that sin and its consequences, because they are all children of Adam.

5. What do we call this sin that comes to us from Adam?

This sin that comes to us from Adam is called original sin.

6. Does our soul die, as our body does?

No, our soul never dies, for it is immortal.

7. What does our soul lose through grave sin?

Through grave sin, our soul loses that divine life which is the Grace of God.

8. What did God do to save men from sin?

To save men from sin, God sent His Son who was made man (Incarnation) and who died on the Cross (Redemption).

WORDS TO THINK ABOUT

"The fall of Adam – a terrible fall which gave entry to sin into the heart of man."

St John Vianney

LESSON 6 – THE MYSTERY OF THE INCARNATION.
JESUS CHRIST

WORDS TO READ

God the Father sent His Son into the world.

This Son –
    Begotten of the Father before all time began,
    God, from God,
    Light, from Light,
    True God, from True God,
    Begotten, not made,
    Consubstantial[1] with the Father,
Through Him all things were made.

    For us men and for our salvation,
    He became incarnate:
    by the power of the Holy Spirit,
    in the womb of the Virgin Mary
    HE BECAME MAN – Jesus Christ.
    That is the mystery of *the Incarnation*.

QUESTIONS AND ANSWERS TO LEARN

1. What is the mystery of the Incarnation?

The mystery of the Incarnation is the mystery of the Son of God made man.

2. Has the Son of God always been man?

No, the Son of God (God the Son) has not always been man: but He has always been God. As God, He had no beginning.

---

1. This means "of one and the same substance or essence". He has the same Divine nature as the Father (translator's note).

3. Did the Son of God stop being God when He became man?

No, the Son of God after the Incarnation is God and man, both together, and He will be so eternally.

4. What is the Son of God, made man, called?

The Son of God, made man, is called Jesus Christ.

5. Has the Son of God always been called Jesus Christ?

No, it is only since He became man that the Son of God is called Jesus Christ.

6. What do you understand when you say that the Son of God became man?

The Son of God became man means that He took our human nature – that is to say, a body and a soul like us.

7. How many natures are there in Jesus Christ?

There are two natures in Jesus Christ: the Divine nature and the human nature.

8. How many Persons are there in Jesus Christ?

There is only one single Person in Jesus Christ who is God the Son, the Second Person of the Holy Trinity.

9. Why did the Son of God so lower Himself as to become man?

The Son of God so lowered Himself as to become man because He wanted to suffer in order to save us.

WORDS TO THINK ABOUT

"By His incarnation, God hides His divinity, so as to become visible to our eyes."

St John Vianney

LESSON 7 – THE BLESSED VIRGIN MARY

WORDS TO READ

To make Himself man, the Son of God wished to have, like us, a mother.

He chose the wholly-pure Virgin Mary.

To prepare her to become His mother, He preserved Mary from original sin: that is *the Immaculate Conception*.

God sent the archangel Gabriel to say to Mary: "You are full of grace. The Lord is with you; blessed are you among all women. You will bear a child who will be the Son of God!" The archangel was asking for her consent to this.

Mary replied: "I am the servant of the Lord; let it be done to me according to His will."

At that moment, the Son of God became incarnate, became man: He is called Jesus.

Mary is the Mother of God, because her Child is the Son of God – true God and true man at the same time.

Mary is *our* Mother, because the Son of God came on earth to save all men, all human beings.

Born of the Virgin Mary, the Son of God had no father upon earth. St Joseph, the husband of Mary, was chosen by God to protect the Child-God and His mother.

QUESTIONS AND ANSWERS TO LEARN

1. Where did Jesus Christ become man?

Jesus Christ became man in the womb of the Blessed Virgin Mary.

2. Who fashioned the body of Jesus in the womb of the Blessed Virgin?

It was the power of the Holy Spirit that fashioned the body of Jesus in the womb of the Blessed Virgin.

3. Therefore, St Joseph is not the father of Jesus?

No, St Joseph is not the father of Jesus, for the Son of God made man had no father upon earth.

4. Did the Blessed Virgin Mary stop being a virgin in becoming the mother of the Son of God?

No, Mary has always remained a virgin, even in becoming the mother of the Son of God. That is a miracle of the Holy Spirit.

5. On what day did the Son of God become man?

The Son of God became man when the Blessed Virgin replied "Yes" to the archangel Gabriel. That was the day of the Annunciation, which we celebrate on March 25th.

6. Why do we call Mary "the Mother of God"?

We call Mary "the Mother of God" because she is the mother of a Son who is God.

7. Why do we call Mary our mother?

We call Mary our mother because she is the mother of all men, of all human beings, whom Jesus came to save.

8. Why do we call Mary herself the Immaculate Conception?

We call Mary the Immaculate Conception because God preserved Mary from original sin: she was conceived sinless.

WORDS TO THINK ABOUT

"The Blessed Virgin is that beautiful creature who has never displeased the good God."

St John Vianney

LESSON 8 – THE CHILDHOOD OF JESUS

WORDS TO READ

Jesus was born at Bethlehem, a town in Judea, in a poor stable.

It was on Christmas Day, which we celebrate every year on December 25th.

The name Jesus, given to the Son of God made man, means "Saviour", because Jesus came on earth to "save" the fallen human race. His redeeming death gave people the possibility of going to Heaven to enjoy eternal happiness there.

Ever since the great promise of a Saviour to come, people were awaiting the Messiah (that is to say, the *Anointed One*).

After His birth, the Child Jesus was adored by local shepherds. Later, He received the visit of the three Wise Men, who came from the East.

During His childhood, Jesus obeyed Mary and Joseph. He laboured as a carpenter in St Joseph's workshop.

QUESTIONS AND ANSWERS TO LEARN

1. On what day was Our Lord Jesus Christ born?

Our Lord Jesus Christ was born on Christmas Day, which we celebrate on December 25th.

2. What does the name Jesus mean?

The name Jesus means Saviour.

3. Where was Jesus born?

Jesus was born at Bethlehem, a little town in Judea, in a poor stable.

4. By whom was Jesus adored?

Jesus was adored first by shepherds of the locality, and later by the Wise Men who had come from the East.

5. What was Jesus's life during His childhood?

Jesus was obedient to Mary and Joseph, and he carried out the trade of carpenter.

WORDS TO THINK ABOUT

"What did the Blessed Virgin and St Joseph do? They looked after, they contemplated, they admired the Child Jesus. That was the whole of their occupation."

St John Vianney

LESSON 9 – THE PUBLIC LIFE OF JESUS.

PREACHING. MIRACLES.

WORDS TO READ

When he was about 30, Jesus went out to preach the Gospel.

He declared Himself to be the Son of God; He asked us to love God above all else, and not to offend God by sin.

He also asked us to love one another.

In order to show that He really is the Son of God (that is, God the Son, the eternal uncreated Son of the Father):

- Jesus fulfilled the *prophecies*, occurrences announced in advance by men sent by God, whom we call prophets.

- Jesus *worked miracles*: He raised the dead to life, He produced sudden cures – things which could only happen by a direct intervention of God.

QUESTIONS AND ANSWERS TO LEARN

1. What did Jesus do when He was about 30 years old?

When He was about 30 years old, Jesus travelled through towns and villages preaching the Gospel.

2. What did Jesus say?

Jesus said:
- that He was the Son of God, sent by His Father,
- that we ought to love God above all else, and not to offend God by sin,
- that we ought to love one another.

3. How did Jesus show that He was the Son of God?

Jesus showed that He was the Son of God:
- by fulfilling the prophecies,
- by working miracles.

4. What is a prophecy?

A prophecy is something foretold, which later happens.

5. What is a miracle?

A miracle is something which takes place outside the natural order, through a special intervention of God: for example, the instantaneous curing of a fracture or of a very grave organic illness.

WORDS TO THINK ABOUT

"The good God works miracles even now."

St John Vianney

LESSON 10 – THE MYSTERY OF THE REDEMPTION:

Death of Jesus Christ

WORDS TO READ

The Son of God, made man, offered Himself up in sacrifice to save the fallen human race. His redeeming death won for everyone the possibility of going to Heaven. That is the Mystery of the Redemption.

Jesus died on the Cross, at Jerusalem, on Good Friday.

Because He is God the Son, His offering had an infinite value, and therefore His death was capable of making up for the gravity of sin.

Upon the Cross, Jesus brought to our minds that Mary is our mother now. To do that, He entrusted her to St John, saying to her: "This is your son." Then He said to St John: "This is your mother."

Jesus's soul, separated from His body at death, went down to hell[1] to announce to the just their deliverance.

Jesus's body was placed in a tomb, awaiting the Resurrection.

Jesus's Divinity remained united to His soul and to His body.

---

1. "This 'hell' was different from the hell of the damned. It was the state of all those, righteous and evil, who died before Christ" (Compendium of the Catechism of the Catholic Church, para. 125).

QUESTIONS AND ANSWERS TO LEARN

1. What is the mystery of the Redemption?

The mystery of the Redemption is the mystery of Jesus Christ dying on the Cross to redeem the human race.

2. How did Jesus Christ die?

Jesus Christ was crucified at Jerusalem, upon Mount Calvary, on Good Friday.

3. Why did Our Lord Jesus Christ wish to suffer so cruel a death?

Jesus Christ wished to suffer so cruel a death to show us the full generosity of His love.

4. Why do you say that Jesus died on the Cross?

I say that Jesus died on the Cross because the soul of Jesus was separated from His body.

5. What became of the soul of Jesus?

The soul of Jesus went down to hell[1] to await the Resurrection and to announce to the just their deliverance.

6. What became of the body of Jesus?

The body of Jesus was taken down from the Cross and placed in the tomb.

7. What became of the Divinity of Jesus?

The Divinity of Jesus remained always united to His soul and to His body.

---

1. See note on page 43.

WORDS TO THINK ABOUT

"The Blessed Virgin has given birth to us twice – in the Incarnation and at the foot of the Cross. She is therefore our mother twice over!"

St John Vianney

LESSON 11 – THE MYSTERY OF THE REDEMPTION:

Resurrection and Ascension

WORDS TO READ

On the Third Day, Easter Sunday, Jesus rose from the dead.

Some holy women, going to the tomb, found it empty. Two angels were there and spoke to them. The big stone that formed the door of the tomb had been rolled back. The linen cloths which had wrapped Jesus's body were inside the empty tomb.

Jesus, glorious, appeared to His apostles, and remained with them for forty days.

At the end of that time, He ascended (went up) to Heaven. That was Ascension Day, which we celebrate each year, forty days after Easter.

Henceforth Jesus is present in Heaven in the glory of His Father, and is present to us on earth in a special way. The Holy Eucharist (Blessed Sacrament) is Jesus Himself under the appearances of bread and wine.

QUESTIONS AND ANSWERS TO LEARN

1. Did Our Lord Jesus Christ always stay dead?
No, Our Lord Jesus Christ did not always stay dead. On the third day He rose from the dead, glorious.

2. On what day did Jesus rise from the dead?
Jesus rose from the dead on Easter Sunday.

3. What became of Jesus after His resurrection?

Forty days after His resurrection, Jesus ascended to Heaven.

4. On what day did Jesus ascend to Heaven?

Jesus went up to Heaven on Ascension Day.

5. Was it as God that Our Lord Jesus Christ was born of the Blessed Virgin Mary, suffered, died, rose from the dead, and ascended to Heaven?

No, it was as man that Our Lord Jesus Christ was born of the Blessed Virgin Mary, suffered, died, rose from the dead, and ascended to Heaven.

6. Then, what is the reason why the death and sufferings of Jesus are of such great merit?

The death and sufferings of Jesus are of such great merit because the same Person who suffered and died as man is also truly God.

7. Where is Jesus Christ now?

Jesus Christ is in Heaven, and He is present to us on earth in a special way. The Holy Eucharist (Blessed Sacrament) is Jesus Himself under the appearances of bread and wine.

WORDS TO THINK ABOUT

"He died for all: He is waiting for us all in heaven!"
St John Vianney

LESSON 12 – THE HOLY SPIRIT

WORDS TO READ

Before going up into heaven, Jesus Christ promised His apostles that He would send them the Holy Spirit, the Third Person of the Holy Trinity (Jn 14:26; 15:26; 16:7).

The Holy Spirit makes Himself known as the Love of the Father for the Son, and of the Son for the Father. He comes into the world to continue the work of the Son.

The role of the Holy Spirit is to make us understand what Jesus taught, to enlighten us, to guide us, to give us strength. He is the "Teacher inside us": He is called the Consoler ("Paraclete"), the Spirit of Truth.

QUESTIONS AND ANSWERS TO LEARN

1. What grace did Jesus Christ give to His Church after having gone up into heaven?

Jesus Christ, after having gone up into heaven, sent the Holy Spirit to His Church.

2. Who is the Holy Spirit?

The Holy Spirit is the Third Person of the Holy Trinity. He is God as the Father and the Son are. The Three (Father, Son and Holy Spirit) are one single God.

3. What is the role of the Holy Spirit?

The role of the Holy Spirit is to sanctify and govern the Church. He inspires us, enlightens us and guides us.

4. Did Jesus promise the coming of the Holy Spirit?

Yes. Jesus promised His Apostles that they would receive the Holy Spirit "who will teach you all things" (Jn 14:26).

WORDS TO THINK ABOUT

"When the Holy Spirit wills something, He is always successful."

St John Vianney

LESSON 13 – THE CHURCH. THE POPE

WORDS TO READ

Before going up again to His Father, Jesus founded His Church. (It is sometimes described as the *People of God.*)

For this, He chose St Peter as head of the apostles and charged him with governing the Church.

Peter had been called Simon, but Jesus gave him the name "Peter" (a word which means "rock") and said to him: "You are Peter, and upon this rock I will build my Church: and the gates of hell shall not prevail against it" (Mt 16:18).

Jesus also said to him: "Feed my lambs, feed my sheep" (Jn 21:15-17). So St Peter became the shepherd of the clergy and of the faithful.

The Pope is the successor of St Peter, and the bishops are the successors of the apostles.

When the Pope defines truths concerning faith or morals, he cannot be mistaken. The name for this is *infallibility.*

QUESTIONS AND ANSWERS TO LEARN

1. What is the Church?

The Church is the body of all the faithful, united by the same faith and the same sacraments, under the guidance of our Holy Father the Pope and the bishops united to the Pope.

2. Who founded the Church?

It was Jesus Christ who founded the Church. He gave Simon the name "Peter" (meaning "Rock") and said to him: "You are Peter, and upon this rock I will build my Church: and the gates of hell shall not prevail against it."

3. Who is the Head of the Church?

Our Lord Jesus Christ is the invisible Head of the Church, and upon earth the Pope is the visible head of it.

4. Who is the Pope?

The Pope is the successor of St Peter, charged with governing the Church.

5. Who are the bishops?

The bishops are the successors of the apostles, charged with governing dioceses, in union with the Pope.

6. Can the Pope be mistaken?

The Pope cannot be mistaken when he defines truths concerning faith or morals. When doing this, he is infallible.

7. What is the cause of this infallibility of the Pope?

The cause of the infallibility of the Pope is the help of the Holy Spirit, in consequence of the promise made by Jesus Christ to St Peter.

8. How many Churches are there?

Only one Church was founded by Jesus Christ. It is the One, Holy, Catholic and Apostolic Church.[1]

> **WORDS TO THINK ABOUT**
>
> *"Happy the Christian who is well instructed, and who enters into the spirit of the Church."*
>
> St John Vianney

---

1. *Translator's note for teachers:*
   For short summaries of "One", "Holy", "Catholic" and "Apostolic" as marks of the Church, see P/Ctm, paras. 94-99; H/P, p. 35. St Peter, whom Christ made the visible head of His Church on earth, preached and was martyred *at Rome.* He was the first Bishop of Rome. The divine authority and assistance given to Peter for safeguarding the unity of the Church and the true teaching delivered to the Apostles, applies to St Peter's successors also. After Peter's death, his successors as Pope (also called "Roman Pontiff") were Linus, and on his death, Cletus, and on his death, Clement I; and so on, all the way to our present Pope.

LESSON 14 – THE MEMBERS OF THE CHURCH

WORDS TO READ

The members of the Church whose souls have been sanctified by divine life are united with each other. This is the Communion of Saints.

First, there are those who have reached the happiness of Heaven. They are the *Church Triumphant.* Having won their victory, they intercede with God for us.

Next, those who, awaiting their entry into Heaven, are being purified in Purgatory. This is the *Church Suffering.* We should pray for them.

Lastly, we upon earth have to struggle, to fight, in order to remain faithful to God. We form the *Church Militant.* We should pray for all our brothers and sisters of the Church Militant – in particular, those who live in a state of sin.

QUESTIONS AND ANSWERS TO LEARN

1. What is the Church Triumphant?

Those who have already reached Heaven form the Church Triumphant.

2. What is the Church Suffering?

Those who await their entry into Heaven and are still completing their sanctification in Purgatory form the Church Suffering.

3. What is the Church Militant?

Those who, upon earth, struggle in order to win victory over evil. These form the Church Militant.

4. What is the Communion of Saints?

The Communion of Saints is the union, through prayer, of all the members of the Church: in Heaven, in Purgatory, and on earth.

WORDS TO THINK ABOUT

"What a beautiful union there is between the Church on earth and the Church in Heaven! As St Teresa of Avila said: 'You in triumphing, we in fighting – we make up but one for glorifying God.'"

St John Vianney

LESSON 15 – THE FORGIVENESS OF SINS

WORDS TO READ

Forgiveness of sins results from Jesus's Sacrifice on the Cross. He has saved us.

Jesus entrusted to His Church the power to forgive sins. Addressing His Apostles, He said to them: "Receive the Holy Spirit. Whose sins you shall forgive, those sins are forgiven them. Whose sins you shall retain, those sins are retained." (Jn 20:22-23)

This power belongs to the bishops and priests, and the pardoning of sins takes place through the Sacrament of Baptism and the Sacrament of Penance:

- Baptism wipes out original sin in the case of a little child and of an adult. (It also wipes out every sin committed by a person before baptism.)

- The Sacrament of Penance (also known as the Sacrament of Reconciliation) gives us pardon of all sins that we confess. We can receive this sacrament throughout our life.

Those who, through no fault of their own, do not know of or recognize the Church can also be saved if, moved by grace, they try to do God's will to the extent that they know it, and follow the natural law written in their hearts.

QUESTIONS AND ANSWERS TO LEARN

1. Why are our sins pardoned?
Our sins are pardoned because Jesus redeemed us by dying on the Cross.

2. Who received the power to forgive sins?
The Church received the power to forgive sins when Jesus said to His Apostles: "Receive the Holy Spirit. Whose sins you shall forgive, those sins are fogiven them."

3. How does the Church forgive sins?
The Church forgives sins:

– by Baptism, for original sin,

– by the Sacrament of Penance (also known as the Sacrament of Reconciliation) for the sins we ourselves have committed.

4. Can one be saved outside the Church?
All salvation comes from Christ and His Church. But those who, through no fault of their own, do not know of or recognize the Church can be saved if they try to do God's will to the extent that they know it, and follow the natural law.

5. What is the natural law?
The natural law is the law written in the heart of every person for discerning right and wrong.

LESSON 16 – THE RESURRECTION OF THE BODY, AND LAST JUDGEMENT.

LIFE ETERNAL

WORDS TO READ

After death, the souls of all, of everyone, continue to exist, for ever.

If we go to Heaven, we shall live *in eternal happiness.* We shall know another life that we cannot now imagine. As St Paul says: "Eye has not seen, ear has never heard, what God prepares for those who love Him."

The Preface of the Mass of the Dead puts it this way: "Life is not destroyed, but transformed... and our stay on earth is changed to an eternal dwelling-place in Heaven." We shall possess God for ever; this is Life Eternal.

We are judged immediately on death, and this determines where we (our immortal souls) there-upon go (see questions and answers 4 to 7), according to our state of soul at death. And when the end of the world comes, the *bodies* of all who have died (Jn 5:29) will rise and be re-united with their souls. The souls of the holy will receive their bodies gloriously transformed (as Christ's resur-rected body was transformed and is ever-glorious in heaven).

The individual judgement that takes place at death is called the *particular* judgement. At the end of the world, at the Second Coming of Christ, there will be a judgement of *everyone*, both living and dead, called the Last Judgement.

By a special privilege, the sinless Virgin Mary was taken up, *body as well as soul,* into Heaven when the course of her earthly life was finished. This taking up to Heaven is called her Assumption. Her body, which had borne her Maker, did not suffer the corruption of the grave.

QUESTIONS AND ANSWERS TO LEARN

1. What is death?

Death is the separation of body and soul.

2. Does our soul die like our body?

No, our soul does not die like our body, for it is immortal.

3. What becomes of our soul at death?

At death, the soul is judged individually by Our Lord Jesus Christ.

4. Where does the soul go after that judgement?

After that judgement, the soul goes either to Heaven (Paradise), or to Purgatory, or to Hell.

5. What is Heaven?

Heaven (Paradise) is a state of bliss where the souls of the holy are completely happy because they possess God, and will possess God for ever.

6. What is Purgatory?

Purgatory is a state of purification or punishment (lasting only for a time, not for ever) where souls, who have died in a state of grace, complete the expiation of their sins in an ardent desire to enter Heaven and possess God. This they will finally do.

7. What is Hell?

Hell is a state of suffering where the damned are in torment for ever, because they lack God.

8. Can we assist the souls in Purgatory?

Yes, we can assist the souls in Purgatory by our prayers and our good actions.

9. What do we mean by the resurrection of the body?

The resurrection of the body (which will take place at Christ's Second Coming at the end of the world) means that the bodies of those who have died will be restored to life and re-united with their souls, and we shall all of us be judged by Our Lord Jesus Christ. This is called the Last Judgement.

10. What will happen at the Last Judgement?

At the Last Judgement, the conduct of each person, and either their state of acceptance of God's grace, or their state of rejection of it and final impenitence, will be brought to light by Christ the Just Judge.

11. Who will be judged at the Last Judgement?

Everyone will be judged at the Last Judgement, including those still on earth.

12. What is Life Eternal?

Life Eternal (also called Life Everlasting) is the possession of God for ever.

WORDS TO THINK ABOUT

"Our home is above. On earth we are lodging at an inn, just passing through."

St John Vianney

LESSON 17 – THE CREDO or APOSTLES' CREED

WORDS TO READ

All the truths we are going to study are summarized in the Apostles' Creed, or the *Credo* (from the Latin word for "I believe"). This is doctrine taught by Jesus and entrusted to His apostles. The Church is the guardian of this treasure and has to defend it against errors (heresies).

In earlier times adults, before receiving baptism, used to come and declare "I believe..."

On the day of our baptism when we were babies, our godparents affirmed on our behalf: "I believe..."

Each of us renewed the profession of faith, "I believe...", on the occasion of receiving the Sacrament of Confirmation. At the Masses of the Easter Vigil and Easter Day, too, all present are asked to do the same.

Every Sunday, at Mass, we declare "I believe" when we recite the *Credo*. (The *Credo* in the Mass is more developed: it is the Nicene Creed, drawn up at the time of a Council of the Church.)

With the whole Church, let us love to say or sing that *Credo*.

QUESTIONS AND ANSWERS TO LEARN

1. Where is the summary of the truths taught by Jesus Christ contained?

A summary of the truths taught by Jesus Christ is contained in the *Credo* or Apostles' Creed.

2. What were the apostles?

The apostles were twelve men chosen by Jesus to follow Him and to continue His mission.

3. What is the Apostles' Creed?

The Apostles' Creed is a short summary of the truths we ought to believe. These truths are the basis of our doctrine.

4. Where does the word *Credo* come from?

The word Credo is the first word of the Creed: in Latin it means "I believe…"

5. Let us now proclaim our Faith through the *Credo*:

1. I believe in God the Father Almighty, Creator of Heaven and Earth.
2. I believe in Jesus Christ, His only Son, our Lord,
3. who was conceived by the power of the Holy Spirit and was born of the Virgin Mary.
4. He suffered under Pontius Pilate, was crucified, died, and was buried.
5. He descended into hell.[1] On the third day He rose again.
6. He ascended into heaven and is seated at the right hand of the Father.
7. From there, He will come again to judge the living and the dead.
8. I believe in the Holy Spirit,
9. the Holy Catholic Church,
10. the Communion of Saints,
11. the forgiveness of sins,
12. the resurrection of the body,
13. and Life Everlasting. Amen.

---

1. See page 43 above.

WORDS TO THINK ABOUT

"Through Faith we believe what God has promised: we believe that we shall see Him one day, that we shall possess Him, that we shall be eternally with Him in Heaven."

St John Vianney

BOOK TWO

GRACE AND
THE SACRAMENTS

LESSON 1 – GRACE

WORDS TO READ

Jesus said to His apostles: "I am the Vine, and you are the branches (the vine-shoots)."

Now, the branches must remain united to the trunk in order to receive the *sap*. A branch separated from the trunk is dead!

In a similar way, Jesus gives us *grace*. This is a Divine life which flows in us as the sap flows into the branches.

Let us remember the promise of Jesus: "If anyone loves me, my Father will love him and we shall come to him and make our dwelling in him."

Jesus said also: "Without me, you can do nothing."

We must guard within us that spiritual life, we must remain always in a *state of grace*. Then we can say, as St Paul did: "It is no longer I who live, it is Christ who lives in me."

QUESTIONS AND ANSWERS TO LEARN

1. What is grace?

Grace is a gift from God which makes us share in the Divine life as children of God – sons and daughters of the Father, brothers and sisters of Jesus, and temples of the Holy Spirit.

2. Is grace necessary?

Yes, grace is necessary for becoming holy and meriting heaven.

3. What do we call this grace that makes us share in the Divine life?

This grace that makes us share in the Divine life is called sanctifying grace. Having it, we are in are "in a state of grace".

4. How do we receive sanctifying grace?

We receive sanctifying grace through the sacraments of Baptism and Penance.

5. Can we lose grace?

Yes, we lose grace through mortal sin.

6. Do we receive other graces?

Yes, we receive other graces, the "actual graces". These are helps that God sends us to aid us to do good.

WORDS TO THINK ABOUT

"A Christian created in the image of God.
A Christian redeemed by the blood of One
who is God. A Christian –
God's child,
God's brother (or sister),
God's heir!

St John Vianney

LESSON 2 – THE SACRAMENTS

WORDS TO READ

The sacraments are outward signs instituted by Jesus Christ in order to give us inward grace.

There are three elements in a sacrament:

1. The things that play the part of *matter* (for example, the *water* of baptism),

2 . The words that play the part of *form* (for example, the form of words "I baptize you in the name of the Father and of the Son and of the Holy Spirit"),

3. The person of the "*minister* of the sacrament", who confers the sacrament with the intention of doing what the Church does.

What a wonderful method devised by Our Lord Jesus Christ! The sacraments are for the purpose of giving us grace, or of increasing grace in our souls.

Thus, the Sacrament of Baptism and the Sacrament of Penance *give* grace: we call them "sacraments of the dead" (because they give spiritual life).

The other sacraments have to be received in a "state of grace": we call them "sacraments of the living".

Further, each of the sacraments has its own particular grace that differentiates it from the other sacraments.

Certain sacraments imprint upon the soul an indelible character – that is to say, a mark which will exist always. That is the case with Baptism, with Confirmation, with Holy Orders.

The sacraments have their source in the Sacrifice of Jesus Christ on the Cross. That is why they have been compared to channels through which the blood of Jesus flows and is received by us individually.

The sacraments are *entrusted to the Church.* She, the Church, distributes them to us.

The sacraments are the *treasure* of the Church.

The sacraments are what *makes the greatness of the priest.* It is he who gives the sacraments in the name of Jesus Christ.

The first sacrament to receive is Baptism, for it gives us divine life.

The greatest of the sacraments is the Holy Eucharist, for it gives, not only grace but Him who is the *Giver and Source* of grace. This Sacrament consists of the real and substantial presence of Our Lord Jesus Christ. That is why it is called the Blessed Sacrament.

QUESTIONS AND ANSWERS TO LEARN

1. What is a sacrament?

A sacrament is a sign, by action and words, instituted by Our Lord Jesus Christ in order to produce or increase grace.

2. How many sacraments are there?

There are *seven* sacraments:
–   Baptism,
–   Confirmation,
–   The Holy Eucharist,
–   Penance (Reconciliation),

- Anointing of the Sick,
- Holy Orders,
- Marriage (Matrimony).

3. What are the elements of a sacrament?

A sacrament involves three elements:

1. The matter – this is the things used.
2. The form – this is the words.
3. The minister of the sacrament – the person who confers the sacrament with the intention of doing what the Church does.

4. Which are the sacraments that GIVE grace?

The sacraments that GIVE grace are Baptism and Penance. They are called "sacraments of the dead" because they give spiritual life or give it back when it has been lost.

5. Which are the sacraments that INCREASE grace?

The sacraments that INCREASE grace are those that one has to receive in a state of grace: they are called "sacraments of the living". These sacraments are: Confirmation, Holy Eucharist, Anointing of the Sick, Holy Orders and Marriage.

6. Which are the sacraments that someone can receive only once?

The sacraments that someone can receive only once are: Baptism, Confirmation and Holy Orders, because they imprint on our soul an indelible character – that is to say, a mark that can never be removed.

7. Which is the greatest of the sacraments?

The greatest of the sacraments is the Holy Eucharist, for it consists not only of grace but of the Giver and Source of grace, Our Lord Jesus Christ, really and substantially present.

WORDS TO THINK ABOUT

"Those who go to the sacraments will not all be saints, but there will always be saints amongst those receiving the sacraments."

St John Vianney

LESSON 3 – BAPTISM

WORDS TO READ

As we have said, Baptism is the first sacrament, the one that opens the door, that permits us to receive the others. Indeed, this sacrament gives grace to us, by virtue of the merits of Jesus Christ who died upon the Cross to save us.

It is a great fault to delay without reason the baptism of a little child! The Church never ceases to remind us of this.

Baptism wipes out original sin, and makes us a Christian, a child of God and of the Church.

When an adult receives Baptism, he obtains pardon of all the sins he may have committed previously, provided he (or she) is sorry for them.

The *matter* of Baptism is the water that flows over the head of the person baptised.

The *form* consists of the words spoken by the priest: "I baptize you in the name of the Father and of the Son and of the Holy Spirit."

The usual minister of the Sacrament is the priest, but in the case of urgency, in the absence of a priest, any person can baptize. That is allowed because of the importance of the Sacrament of Baptism.

Baptism is necessary for salvation, but certain circumstances can take the place of it for the salvation of the individual concerned. Those circumstances are:

1. Someone suffers death for the faith, is martyred. That is baptism *of blood.*

2. Someone dies in the love of God, wishing for baptism but unable to receive it. That is one example of baptism *of desire.*[1]

QUESTIONS AND ANSWERS TO LEARN

1. What is Baptism?

Baptism is a sacrament that wipes out original sin, and gives grace to us. It makes us a Christian, a child of God and of the Church.

2. Is it necessary to be baptized?

Baptism is necessary for salvation for those to whom the Gospel has been proclaimed and who have had the possibility of asking for this sacrament.[2]

3. Who is the minister of the Sacrament of Baptism?

The minister of the Sacrament of Baptism is the priest, but any person can baptize in case of necessity.

4. What must the priest do in order to baptize?

To baptize, the priest must pour water upon the head of the child, and at the same time say the words: "I baptize you in the name of the Father and of the Son and of the Holy Spirit".

---

1. Concerning those seeking truth and doing God's will as they know it, though ignorant of the Gospel, see full CCC, para. 1260.
2. See further CCC, paras. 1257-1261; Cpend, paras. 261-262.

5. What are the baptismal promises that the child will renew later?

The baptismal promises that the child will renew later are:

1. I reject Satan and sin.
2. I believe in God the Father.
3. I believe in Jesus Christ, His only Son, our Lord.
4. I believe in the Holy Spirit.
5. I believe in the Holy Catholic Church, the communion of saints, the forgiveness of sins, the resurrection of the body, and Life Everlasting.

6. Does baptism wipe out original sin only?

No, baptism received by one who has reached the age of reason (generally regarded as a person over seven years old) wipes out all sins committed before receiving this sacrament.

7. Can other things take the place of baptism?

Yes. Those other things are:

1. Someone dies a martyr for the faith. That is baptism of blood.

2. Someone dies in the love of God, wishing for baptism but unable to receive it. That is one example of baptism of desire.

WORDS TO THINK ABOUT

"If we understood what it is to be a child of God, we would not be able to do evil, we would be like angels on earth."

St John Vianney

LESSON 4 – CONFIRMATION

WORDS TO READ

The Sacrament of Confirmation comes to us to give us an increase of strength and of light, for the Holy Spirit invades our soul to help us in this way.

The grace of this Sacrament is that of making us stronger to fight against evil and defend our faith.

It is often said that Confirmation makes us a soldier of Christ. This is to show that we must be armed against the devil. St Paul compares our life to a battle, in which we have to struggle like a soldier who wears armour and is equipped with shield and sword.

We have already received the Holy Spirit at our baptism, but He comes again, and brings us His gifts: *Wisdom*, *Understanding*, *Counsel* (right judgement), *Fortitude* (strength and courage), *Knowledge*, *Piety* (loving reverence for God), and *Fear of the Lord* (loving dread of offending God).

Thereafter, we shall be witnesses to Jesus Christ, charged with testifying to our faith, through our words and our actions.

Confirmation imprints in us an indelible, a permanent, character. That is what is signified by the anointing of our forehead – an anointing with holy chrism by the bishop (or by a priest whom the bishop has authorised to give Confirmation). This sacrament can only be received one single time.

QUESTIONS AND ANSWERS TO LEARN

1. What is Confirmation?

Confirmation is a sacrament which gives us the Holy Spirit with the abundance of His gifts, and makes us a complete Christian, a witness to and a soldier of Christ and His Church.

2. What are the gifts of the Holy Spirit?

The gifts of the Holy Spirit are: *Wisdom*, *Understanding*, *Counsel* (right judgement), *Fortitude* (strength and courage), *Knowledge*, *Piety* (loving reverence for God), and *Fear of the Lord* (loving dread of offending God).

3. Who is the minister of the Sacrament of Confirmation?

The minister of the Sacrament of Confirmation is the bishop, a successor of the apostles; but the bishop can also authorize one of his priests to give Confirmation.

4. How does the bishop give Confirmation?

To give Confirmation, the bishop stretches out his hands over those who are to be confirmed, and calls upon the Holy Spirit. Then he anoints the forehead of each one of them with holy chrism, while uttering the prescribed words.

5. What is holy chrism?

Holy chrism is a mixture of olive oil and balm which the bishop, on Holy Thursday, has dedicated for this use.

6. What is the effect of Confirmation?

Confirmation gives us the strength to witness boldly to our faith.

WORDS TO THINK ABOUT

"Without the Holy Spirit we are like a crippled man, deprived of the power of moving his limbs. With the Holy Spirit we have strength and power of movement. It is only the Holy Spirit who can lift up a soul and carry that soul up on high."

St John Vianney

LESSON 5 – THE HOLY EUCHARIST (Blessed Sacrament)

WORDS TO READ

The Holy Eucharist (Blessed Sacrament) is the greatest of the sacraments, for it not only gives us grace; it IS the very Source of grace – He who gives grace, Our Lord Jesus Christ.

Under the appearances of bread and wine in this Sacrament, *Jesus is present, really and substantially with His Body, His Blood, His Soul and His Divinity.*

"O majestic Sacrament! Beneath the humble Host, I adore God, true Bread of Life."

We can never thank our loving God enough for having given us this Sacrament!

A Swiss cardinal, who never ceased emphasising the doctrine on the Eucharist, one day wrote about this Sacrament: "Make Jesus known and loved – and the quite amazing love He shows us by remaining in the midst of us."

QUESTIONS AND ANSWERS TO LEARN

1. What is the Holy Eucharist?
The Holy Eucharist is a Sacrament that consists really and substantially of the Body, the Blood, the Soul and the Divinity of Our Lord Jesus Christ, under the appearances of bread and wine.

2. How does the Holy Eucharist become present?

It is at the Sacrifice of the Mass that the Holy Eucharist becomes present.

3. What is the Sacrifice of the Mass?

The Sacrifice of the Mass is Jesus's Sacrifice on the Cross which Jesus continues to offer for us through His priest at the altar.

4. Who instituted the Eucharist?

It was Jesus Himself who instituted the Eucharist, on Holy Thursday, the evening before His death. He took bread, blessed it, broke it, and gave it to His apostles, saying: "Take and eat, this is my Body." He took the cup of wine, blessed the wine and gave it to His apostles, saying: "Take and drink, this is my Blood." Then He added: "Do this in memory of me."

5. At which point in the Mass are the bread and wine changed into Jesus Himself?

It is at the Consecration that this change takes place. The priest repeats the words of Jesus, and it is then that the bread becomes the Body of Jesus and the wine becomes the Blood of Jesus. This is *transubstantiation.*

6. Does any bread and wine remain after the Consecration?

No, after the Consecration no bread and no wine remain in fact; their substance has gone completely. Only their *appearances* remain – that is to say, their shape, their colour and their taste.

7. Is Jesus, whole and entire, under each of the species (appearances) of bread and wine?

Yes. Jesus, whole and entire, is under the species of bread; and, whole and entire, under the species of wine. He is there whole and entire because, living and immortal, His Body, His Blood, His Soul and His Divinity can no longer be separated.

8. Has each little fragment of the consecrated Host been changed into Jesus Himself?

Yes. Even the smallest fragment of the consecrated Host has been changed into Jesus Himself.

WORDS TO THINK ABOUT

"There is nothing greater than the Eucharist!"

St John Vianney

LESSON 6 – THE HOLY SACRIFICE OF THE MASS

WORDS TO READ

When Jesus instituted the Eucharist, on the evening of Holy Thursday, He announced and began His Sacrifice.

He added: "Do this in memory of me." By these words he gave Holy Orders to His apostles (as to the bishops and other priests of today) empowering and commanding them to offer, in His name, the Sacrifice of the Mass.

Each time the priest says Mass, Jesus offers to God His Father, by and through the hands of the priest, His Body and His Blood under the species (appearances) of bread and wine.

Therefore, we can say that:

1. The Mass is a *remembrance* of the Sacrifice of the Cross. The separate consecration of the bread and of the wine recalls the separation of Jesus's Body and Blood on the Cross.

2 . But this memorial is infinitely more than a mere recollection of past events. Mysteriously but really, the Mass *makes truly present* the very same Sacrifice of the Cross that was offered, once and for all, on Calvary. On our altars Jesus continues to offer Himself to the Father, but now through the ministry of priests, and in a manner involving no bloodshed.

3. The Mass applies to us the merits of the Sacrifice of the Cross. At each Mass, God the Father grants us graces merited by Jesus's sacrificial death.

We offer the Sacrifice of the Mass to the Father, and for the following reasons:
- to adore Him,
- to thank Him,
- to ask for new graces,
- to obtain pardon for our sins.

Those are what we call the four ends (objects) of the Sacrifice.

QUESTIONS AND ANSWERS TO LEARN

1. What is the role of the Sacrifice of the Mass?

Besides being a remembrance of the Sacrifice of the Cross, the Mass makes truly present the Sacrifice of the Cross and applies its merits to us.

2. How does the Sacrifice of the Mass make truly present the Sacrifice of the Cross?

The Sacrifice of the Mass makes the Sacrifice of the Cross be truly present because at all Masses Jesus, present on the altar, continues to offer to His Father , through His priests, the Sacrifice He made on Calvary.

3. How does the Sacrifice of the Mass apply the merits of the Sacrifice of the Cross to us?

The Sacrifice of the Mass applies the merits of the Sacrifice of the Cross to us because, at each Mass, God the Father grants to us graces merited by Jesus on the Cross.

4. To whom is the Sacrifice of the Mass offered?

The Sacrifice of the Mass is offered to God the Father, since it is the same Sacrifice as that which on Calvary Jesus, God the Son made man, offered to His Heavenly Father through the Holy Spirit.

5. Why do we offer the Sacrifice of the Mass?

We offer to God the Father the Sacrifice of the Mass:

1. to acknowledge and adore Him as our Sovereign Lord,
2. to thank Him for His benefits,
3. to ask for the graces we need,
4. to obtain pardon for our sins.

WORDS TO THINK ABOUT

(God the Father) "who is so good, cannot refuse us anything if we offer to Him His Son and the merits of His Son's holy death and suffering."

St John Vianney

LESSON 7 – HOLY COMMUNION

WORDS TO READ

When He instituted the Eucharist (Blessed Sacrament), Jesus said: "Take and eat." He desires to give Himself to us, to be the food of our soul: that is *Holy Communion.*

In order to participate better in the Sacrifice of the Mass, it is good to *go to Communion* ("communicate") – that is to say, to receive Jesus, the Blessed Sacrament. Our soul needs that heavenly Food.

As our body needs material food to sustain its natural life, so our soul needs heavenly Food, to nourish its super-natural life in preparation for eternity. Jesus said: "I am the living bread that has come down from heaven", and He also said that "he who eats me will draw life from me." (Jn 6:51, 58). The Blessed Sacrament, that we receive and eat, is indeed Jesus Himself. So amazing a communion with the risen Jesus "preserves, increases and renews the life of grace received at baptism".[1]

We can unfailingly rely on Jesus Christ's promises and the grace of the Sacrament. Communion is itself a pledge of our future glory, since our sacramental union with Christ is a firm token of that indescribable happiness which is offered to us – eternal life in heaven. But we, on our part, have to co-operate with the grace given to us. The grace of Communion strengthens and purifies our desire (and resolve) not

---

1. CCC, para. 1392.

84

to break away from Christ by mortal sin – and especially to desire that we be in a state of grace at the supremely important moment of our bodily death.

One must go to Communion each year at Easter time, and should also receive Communion at the hour of death in order to be better prepared. But, if we want to be faithful to Jesus in the midst of this world, we will seek to receive Him very often, since one can go to Communion every day!

Communion is our whole strength. The holy Curé of Ars, St John Vianney, had well understood this when he wrote: *"If only we knew the value of Communion!"*

QUESTIONS AND ANSWERS TO LEARN

1. Why did Our Lord Jesus Christ wish to be present to us as the Blessed Sacrament?

Our Lord Jesus Christ wanted to be present to us as the Blessed Sacrament:

1. to be offered to God the Father in sacrifice for us in the Holy Mass,
2. to be the food of our souls,
3. to be the object of our adoration.

2. Can the Eucharist be called the Sacrament of Love?

Yes, the Eucharist can be called the Sacrament of Love, because Jesus has shown us an amazing love by remaining in the midst of us.

3. What is "going to Communion"?

Going to Communion is receiving Jesus, the Blessed Sacrament.

4. What are the effects of Communion?

These are the effects of Communion:

– It unites us intimately with Jesus and increases in us the life of grace;

– It weakens our inclination towards evil;

– It is a pledge of our future glory in Life Eternal.

5. What is necessary for going to Communion worthily?

In order to go to Communion worthily, it is necessary:

1. to be in a state of grace (anyone who is conscious of having committed a mortal sin must first go to Confession before receiving Communion), and

2. to have been fasting (no food or drink) for one hour. (Water, however, does not break the fast.)

6. When must we go to Communion?

One must go to Communion at least once a year, at Easter time, and should receive Communion when in danger of death.

7. When can we go to Communion?

We can go to Communion every day if we wish.

WORDS TO THINK ABOUT

"Come to Communion,
Come to Jesus,
Come to live on Him.
so as to live for Him!"

St John Vianney

LESSON 8 – THE SACRAMENT OF PENANCE, or of RECONCILIATION

WORDS TO READ

The Sacrament of Penance (or of Reconciliation) has been instituted by Jesus to grant us forgiveness and reconcile us with God when we fall into any sin.

Jesus, after His resurrection, breathed upon His Apostles and said to them: "Receive the Holy Spirit. Whose sins you shall forgive, those sins are forgiven them; whose sins you shall retain, those sins are retained."

The minister of this Sacrament is the priest approved by the bishop to hear confessions. When the priest grants the pardon, he does it in the name of Jesus, saying: "I absolve you from your sins". But that pardon (absolution) comes to us from the merits of Jesus on the Cross.

Receiving the Sacrament of Penance, also called the Sacrament of Reconciliation, is obligatory for all grave (mortal) sins – sins which destroy the state of grace in our soul.

So as really to receive this Sacrament, it is necessary to be sorry for our sins, to tell them to the priest, to receive absolution, and to make reparation for the wrong done to God and to our neighbour.

QUESTIONS AND ANSWERS TO LEARN

1. What is the Sacrament of Penance?

Penance is a sacrament instituted by Jesus Christ to reconcile us with God, by granting us forgiveness of our sins.

2. When did Jesus institute the Sacrament of Penance?

Jesus, after His resurrection, instituted the Sacrament of Penance when he breathed upon His Apostles and said to them "Receive the Holy Spirit. Whose sins you shall forgive, those sins are forgiven them. Whose sins you shall retain, those sins are retained."

3. Who is the minister of the Sacrament of Penance?

The minister of the Sacrament of Penance is the priest, approved by the bishop.

4. What must we do to receive the Sacrament of Penance?

To receive the Sacrament of Penance, we must:

1. be sorry for our sins (that is contrition),
2. tell our sins to the priest (that is confession),
3. receive the pardon of the priest (that is absolution), and
4. make reparation for our sins (that is called satisfaction).

WORDS TO THINK ABOUT

"It isn't the sinner who returns to God to ask forgiveness from Him; it's God Himself who runs after the sinner and makes that sinner return to Him."

St John Vianney

LESSON 9 – CONTRITION

WORDS TO READ

The most necessary condition for us to receive forgiveness of our sins is that we have regret, or *contrition.* This regret (being sorry for our sins) requires us to be resolved not to sin again.

There are two sorts of contrition:

1. *Perfect contrition:* In this case we are sorry for the sin because of the infinite goodness of God.

Such contrition obtains forgiveness for us immediately, so that even if we were not able to go to confession before death, our soul would be in a state of grace on our appearing before God.

2. *Imperfect contrition:* In this case we are sorry for the sin for some other reason, such as a fear of hell.

Contrition, however (this imperfect contrition at the very least) is necessary to prepare ourselves to receive the Sacrament of Penance.

So as not to fall again into the sins we have regretted, we ought to have recourse to prayer; make efforts to correct ourselves; and avoid dangerous occasions of sin. Indeed, Jesus said: "The Spirit is willing, but the flesh is weak." He also said: "Watch and pray."

QUESTIONS AND ANSWERS TO LEARN

1. What is contrition?

Contrition is sorrow at having offended God, regret at our sins, with a firm resolution not to sin again.

2. How many sorts of contrition are there?

There are two sorts of contrition: perfect contrition and imperfect contrition.

3. What is perfect contrition?

Perfect contrition is a sorrow at having offended God because He is infinitely good and kind, and because sin displeases Him.

4. What is imperfect contrition?

Imperfect contrition is a sorrow at having offended God caused by the ugliness of sin or by fear of the pains with which God punishes it.

5. What is the effect of perfect contrition?

Perfect contrition justifies us (gives us back the state of grace) even before receiving the Sacrament of Penance, provided we have a desire to receive that Sacrament.

6. What is the effect of imperfect contrition?

Imperfect contrition is only a disposition to receive grace in the Sacrament of Penance.

7. How can we keep to our resolution not to fall again into sin?

We can keep to our resolution not to fall again into sin:

– through prayer, to ask for help from God and from the Virgin Mary,
– through efforts to correct ourselves,
– by avoiding occasions of sin.

8. Make an act of contrition.

"O my God, because you are so good, I am very sorry that I have sinned against you, and by the help of your grace I will not sin again."

WORDS TO THINK ABOUT

"O my God, I am very cross with myself
for having displeased you, disobeyed you.
That displeases me very much, and I want to
do better."

St John Vianney

LESSON 10 – CONFESSION.

SATISFACTION (i.e. penance repairing the damage of sin)

WORDS TO READ

In order to receive the Sacrament of Penance, we must go to confession – that is to say accuse ourselves, before a priest, of the sins we have committed.

Before confession, we must seek out our faults: that is *examination of conscience.* To help us in this we can have before us a list of the Commandments.

We have an obligation to confess grave sins (mortal sins) that we have committed, but it is good to accuse ourselves also of other sins (venial sins) that we have committed, for:

1. accusing ourselves helps us to regret our faults;
2. this regret gives us strength to fight against evil.

A sin that we forget when we go to confession is forgiven, but if it was a mortal sin we must tell it at our next confession.

Pardon for sins requires a reparation. This is the *satisfaction* represented by the prayers that the priest asks us to say as a penance. To make reparation for sin, we must also (if this is reasonably possible):

– in the case of a theft, give back what we stole;
– in the case of a wrong done to someone, apologise;
– in the case of a lie, re-establish the truth.

QUESTIONS AND ANSWERS TO LEARN

1. What is confession?

Confession consists of telling one's sins to an authorised priest in order to receive absolution from him.

2. What ought we to do before confession?

Before confession, we should seek out our sins and be sorry for them.

3. Are we obliged to confess all our sins?

We are obliged to confess all our *mortal* sins, but it is good to confess our other sins also.

4. What is absolution?

Absolution is the pardon that the priest gives us. Under the authority he has from Jesus, the priest takes the place of Jesus and says: "I, in the name of the Father and of the Son and of the Holy Spirit, absolve you from your sins."

5. What is the satisfaction?

The satisfaction consists of our making reparation for our sins.

6. How do we make reparation for our sins?

We can make reparation for our sins:

1. by the penance that the priest gives us to say;
2. by our sacrifices; by our acts done from love; by restoring something to its owner if we have stolen it; by apologising if we have offended our neighbour;
3. by acceptance of the troubles that come to us;
4. through the indulgences of the Church.

WORDS TO THINK ABOUT

"When the priest gives absolution, we need only think of one thing. That is that the blood of the Good God is flowing down on our soul so as to wash it, to purify it, and to make it as beautiful as it was immediately after baptism."

St John Vianney

LESSON 11 – ANOINTING OF THE SICK

WORDS TO READ

Anointing of sick persons has been instituted by Jesus in order to prepare them to die well, and to restore the person to health if that is necessary for the spiritual good of his or her soul.

The full teaching on this sacrament is stated by the apostle St James: "Is anyone among you sick? Let him bring in the priests of the Church and let them pray over him, anointing him with oil in the name of the Lord. And the prayer of faith will save the sick man, and the Lord will raise him up; and if he be in sins, they shall be forgiven him." (James 5:14-15).

Anointing of the sick should be given to sick persons who are in danger of death. This sacrament forgives venial sins and even mortal sins if the sick person is incapable of confessing and has at least imperfect contrition.

Nowadays, anointing of the sick can also be given to a number of the faithful, sick or aged, in the course of community celebrations, for example on the occasion of a pilgrimage.

The priest uses olive oil blessed by the bishop, and does the anointing on the forehead, and on the hands open in an attitude of asking and offering. "Through this holy anointing," says the priest, "may the Lord, in His love and mercy, help you with the grace of the Holy Spirit." And: "May the Lord who frees you from sin save you and raise you up."

QUESTIONS AND ANSWERS TO LEARN

1. What is anointing of the sick?

Anointing of the sick is a sacrament which gives, to a sick person whose life is in danger, spiritual help and sometimes a cure.

2. Who is the minister of anointing of the sick?

The minister of anointing of the sick is the priest.

3. What does the priest do to administer anointing of the sick?

To administer anointing of the sick, the priest uses olive oil that has been blessed by the bishop, and does the anointing on the forehead, and on the hands opened in asking for God's mercy.

4. What are the effects of anointing of the sick?

Anointing of the sick produces several effects:

– it increases grace;
– it comforts the sick person;
– it wipes out sins, if the sick person is sorry for them and is incapable of confessing them;
– sometimes it cures the sick person, if that is for the good of his or her soul.

WORDS TO THINK ABOUT

*"One who suffers with patience gains heaven.
One who suffers with joy is assured of heaven."*

St John Vianney

LESSON 12 – HOLY ORDERS

WORDS TO READ

The Sacrament of Holy Orders consecrates bishops and priests to teach, to celebrate the Sacrifice of the Mass and to administer the sacraments.

Only bishops and priests, because of their Holy Orders, have the power to change the bread and wine at Mass into Jesus Himself.

Holy Orders is a sacrament instituted by Jesus:

1. when He said to His Apostles "Go and teach all nations, baptizing them in the name of the Father and of the Son and of the Holy Spirit.";

2. when He commanded His Apostles to celebrate the Sacrifice of the Mass;

3. when He transmitted to His Apostles the power to forgive sins.

The Apostles transmitted the Sacrament of Holy Orders (priesthood) to their successors: the bishops.

Bishop and priest are different degrees of Holy Orders. Only a bishop has the fullness of the priesthood: he is the minister of the Sacrament of Holy Orders, charged with giving it to the priests (i.e. this sacrament *makes* them priests), and the bishop is also charged with consecrating others chosen as bishops.

A priest is a man who is not like others. In the words of Pope John Paul II, a priest "is a man for others". Consecrated to God, the priest is endowed with a particular dignity. A saying of Jesus has to be remembered too: "You are *in* the world, but you are not *of* the world." Although living in the midst of us, the priest has to remain "a man apart", for he is a minister and instrument of Jesus Christ – Jesus the Mediator between God and human beings.

A bishop can ordain deacons, charged with helping the priests, preaching doctrine, administering baptism and giving Holy Communion.

QUESTIONS AND ANSWERS TO LEARN

1. What is Holy Orders?

Holy Orders is a sacrament which assures the Church of having bishops and priests to carry out the sacred functions: teaching, saying Mass and administering the sacraments.

2. Who is the minister of the Sacrament of Holy Orders?

The minister of the Sacrament of Holy Orders is the bishop, successor of the Apostles.

3. Who can receive the Sacrament of Holy Orders?

A man who is called by God and accepted by the bishop for priestly ordination can receive the Sacrament of Holy Orders.

4. Is the priest a man like other men?

No, the priest is not a man like other men; he is "a man for others" and, consecrated to God, he is a minister of Jesus Christ.

5. Seeing that the priest is consecrated to God, is he a man apart from the world?

Yes. Consecrated to God, he is a man *apart* from the world. In the words of Jesus, he is *in* the world, but not *of* the world.

6. What is a deacon?

A deacon is a man who has received from the bishop the order of the diaconate. He has the authority to preach doctrine, administer baptism and give Holy Communion.

WORDS TO THINK ABOUT

"The priest is a man who takes the place of God, a man who is invested with God's powers."

St John Vianney

LESSON 13 – MARRIAGE (Matrimony)

WORDS TO READ

The Sacrament of Marriage gives to husband and wife the grace to carry out well the duties they have undertaken, towards each other and towards their children.

This is a sacrament which involves a commitment, and demands upon themselves, and therefore it calls for a serious preparation through reflection and through prayer.

The characteristics of marriage are:

1. *Unity,* oneness. A man can have only one wife, and a woman only one husband, for so long as both are living. Husband and wife have become one: "they are no longer two, but one flesh" (Mt 19:6).

2. *Indissolubility,* that it cannot be dissolved. The ties contracted by marriage cannot be broken except by the death of one of the spouses.[1]

That stability is a condition for the happiness both of the two spouses and of their children.

Not everyone is destined for marriage. Some persons consecrate their life to God, as do priests, monks and nuns. Their life of celibacy or virginity is one of very great value, for union with God is then easier.

---

1. But sometimes the circumstances show (and a Church tribunal, after investigation, can declare) the nullity of a marriage, i.e. that a particular marriage was never valid in the eyes of the Church. Among the possible factors is that, for a marriage to be a valid one, both persons must have given free consent to it. Explanations of "free consent" and "nullity" in CCC, paras. 1628-1629 (translator).

Such a life allows the following of what, for them, is a better way to become holy. That is a choice grace. As Jesus said, not everyone can fully understand this, but only "those to whom it has been given".

QUESTIONS AND ANSWERS TO LEARN

1. What is marriage?

Marriage (matrimony) is a sacrament that unites a man and a woman, for them to live a Christian life together and bring up their children in conformity with God's wishes.

2. Who are the ministers of marriage?

The ministers of marriage are the two spouses themselves, who together contract a binding commitment. Where at least one of the persons to be married is a Catholic, they must make their marriage vows in the presence of a Catholic priest.

3. What are the characteristics of marriage?

The characteristics of marriage are unity (oneness) and indissolubility.

4. What does the unity of marriage consist of?

The unity of marriage consists of the fact that, under God's law, a man can have only one wife, and a woman only one husband, for so long as both spouses are living. The two spouses have become one.

5. What does the indissolubility of marriage consist of?

The indissolubility of marriage consists of the fact that the binding ties contracted at marriage cannot be broken except by death.

6. What is to be thought of those who, for love of God, do not marry?

Those who, for love of God, do not marry can give a great value to their life in celibacy or virginity. It may be a better way for them to become holy, through a deeper union with God.

WORDS TO THINK ABOUT

"It is agreement directed towards good that pleases the Good God. He holds in horror agreement directed towards evil."

St John Vianney

BOOK THREE

THE MORAL LAW
THE COMMANDMENTS

LESSON 1 – THE TEN COMMANDMENTS OF GOD

WORDS TO READ

In former times, God had chosen a people so as to prepare the Saviour's coming. To this people God had revealed His Law: that is to say, what He required from His children.

This Law, received by Moses on Mount Sinai, is divided into Ten Commandments.

Jesus reminded us that we have to obey each one of these Commandments. He said: "I have not come to abolish the Law, but to bring it to perfection."

To state this Law more briefly, He declared that the Ten Commandments can be summed up in two:

–   The first: "You shall love the Lord your God with your whole heart, and with your whole soul, and with your whole mind, and with your whole strength."

–   The second: "You shall love your neighbour as yourself."

If you look at a list of the Ten Commandments, you will see that:

–   the first three relate directly to God,

–   the seven following ones relate to our neighbour.

It is our duty to obey the Commandments: they constitute what we call the moral law, or morality.

QUESTIONS AND ANSWERS TO LEARN

1. To be saved, is it enough for Catholics to believe the truths of the Faith and to receive the Sacraments?

To be saved, we Catholics must not only believe the truths of the Faith and receive the Sacraments; we must also obey the God's Commandments and those of the Church.

2. How many Commandments of God are there?

There are Ten Commandments of God; they are called the *Decalogue*.

3. Recite the Ten Commandments of God.

1. You shall worship God, and God only.

2. You shall not take the name of God in vain.

3. Remember to keep Sunday holy.

4. Honour your father and your mother.

5. You shall not kill.

6. You shall not commit adultery (nor impurity).

7. You shall not steal.

8. You shall not bear false witness.

9. You shall not covet your neighbour's wife.

10. You shall not covet your neighbour's goods.

4. How can we divide up the Commandments of God?

We can divide the Commandments of God into two groups. The first three have regard to God directly, and the others have regard to our neighbour.

WORDS TO THINK ABOUT

"Love of God is the first and the greatest of the Commandments. It is, as St Paul says, the fullness of life."

St John Vianney

LESSON 2 – FIRST COMMANDMENT:

You shall worship God, and God only.

WORDS TO READ

Worship God: this is the first of the Commandments!

To worship is to recognise the greatness and the majesty of God.

To worship is to make yourself wholly little before the Creator.

"To worship," said a French Cistercian monk, "is to see God in everything; it is to be conscious of being in His presence; it is to be, in your praying, a child speaking to God as your Father."

Our worship should also be given to Jesus Christ, for He is God, God made man. Therefore He has a right to our worship.

We should, in particular, show this worship towards the *Real Presence,* the Eucharistic Presence of Jesus on our altars. To do that, we should:

1. adore Jesus after our holy communion (our private thanksgiving after communion);

2. come to pray before the tabernacle (visit to the Blessed Sacrament);

3. adore the Sacred Host exposed for us to see on the altar, and receive His blessing (Adoration and Benediction of the Blessed Sacrament);

4. acclaim the Blessed Sacrament carried in procession on the Feast of Corpus Christi.

We WORSHIP only God – the Trinity (Father, Son and Holy Spirit). But we should *honour* the Saints, and especially the Blessed Virgin Mary because of her holiness and because she is the Mother of God and our Mother.

This First Commandment prohibits everything that is contrary to respect for God, and in particular:

- *false religions,* which draw us away from God;
- *superstition:* believing in fortune-telling etc.;
- *idolatry:* worship given to idols (persons or things);
- *spiritism and witchcraft:* everything that puts us in touch with the devil.

QUESTIONS AND ANSWERS TO LEARN

1. What does the First Commandment (You shall worship God, and God only) direct us to do?

The First Commandment (You shall worship God, and God only) directs us to adore God and God alone, and to love God with all our heart.

2. What is worshiping God?

To worship God is to recognise Him as the Creator and Lord of all things, and make oneself wholly little before Him.

3. Should we worship Jesus Christ?

Yes, we should worship Jesus Christ because, like the Father and the Holy Spirit, He is God – God the Son made man. And in consequence we should show this worship to Him present on our altars.

4. What does this First Commandment forbid to us?

The First Commandment prohibits all false religions and all *disordered* love of created persons and things. It forbids everything that puts us in touch with the devil.

5. How should we honour the Blessed Virgin?

We should honour the Blessed Virgin more than all the other Saints, because of her position of honour as Mother of God, and because of her eminent holiness.

6. What are our other duties towards the Blessed Virgin and the Saints?

Our other duties towards the Blessed Virgin and the Saints are:

i.   to ask them for their prayers in our needs;

ii. to imitate them in their virtues.

WORDS TO THINK ABOUT

"We should desire God alone, seek only God."

St John Vianney

LESSON 3 – SECOND AND THIRD COMMANDMENTS:

- **You shall not take the name of God in vain**.
- **Remember to keep Sunday holy**.

WORDS TO READ

The Second Commandment speaks of reverence for the name of God. We should never employ this sacred name lightly, or in words of anger, scorn or impatience.

We are required to fulfil our vows – that is, promises to God made as commitments in solemn form.

We should never utter needless oaths – and especially not false ones.

In certain circumstances, very limited ones, we can be called upon to take an oath, putting us under an obligation to tell the truth totally. For example: someone who is a witness in court.

The Third Commandment lays down that we should reserve one day for God: Sunday (otherwise known as the Sabbath Day). That day should be dedicated to prayer, to devotion and to the service of the Lord. On Sunday we leave off doing our weekly work, so as to take rest and to renew our strength.

The prayer involves, first and foremost, our attendance at Holy Mass.

Devotion can be shown by relaxation with our family, or by such things as charitable visits or religious instruction.

On Sundays we are to refrain from engaging in work or activities that "impede the worship of God and disturb the joy proper to the day of the Lord or the necessary relaxation of mind and body."[1]

On the other hand, *everything that is necessary,* for us or for others, on Sunday is permitted. Such is the case with the family cooking, with the work of a restaurant or hotel, with care of the sick, with garage and breakdown services, with public transport: buses and trains.

The "keeping holy" required for Sunday (especially by attendance at Mass) extends likewise to some feast-days designated by the Church. They are called Holy Days of Obligation. Certain of those feast-days vary from one country to another. In England and Wales, besides every Sunday, they are: Christmas Day, Saints Peter and Paul, the Assumption of the Blessed Virgin Mary and All Saints' Day.

QUESTIONS AND ANSWERS TO LEARN

1. What does the Second Commandment (You shall not take the name of God in vain) direct us to do?

The Second Commandment (You shall not take the name of God in vain) directs us:

– to reverence greatly the name of God,
– to carry out faithfully all the vows we take,
– not to utter needless oaths,
– especially not to say on oath what isn't true.

---

1. Cpend, para. 453.

2. What does the Third Commandment (Remember to keep Sunday holy) direct us to do?

The Third Commandment (Remember to keep Sunday holy) directs us to reserve Sunday for prayer and for the service of God. It directs that it be a day of rest for us.

3. Are certain kinds of work permitted on Sunday?

Yes. Permitted on Sunday are all works of necessity: cooking; restaurant work; care of the sick; garage and breakdown work; public transport, etc.

4. Besides Sundays, what days are to be kept holy?

Besides Sundays, the days to be kept holy (especially by attendance at Mass) are those, called Holy Days of Obligation, indicated by the Church for each country.

WORDS TO THINK ABOUT

*"We should be happy to see Sunday arrive.
We shall then exclaim: "Today I shall occupy
myself with the Good God, I shall really pray,
and shall work for the business of my salvation!"*

St John Vianney

LESSON 4 – FOURTH COMMANDMENT:

Honour your father and your mother.

WORDS TO READ

The Fourth Commandment directs children to love and respect their parents and to obey them. It likewise requires them to obey those who sometimes replace their parents – grandparents, uncles and aunts, teachers.

This Commandment extends to our duties towards all those in authority over us. It is therefore very wide, for we are always dependent on someone in the course of our lives:

- our employers in the service of whom we work;

- the Church and her priests: we owe them respect and help;

- the State and those who govern us. We owe them service of our Country, obedience to laws that are just, and payment of our taxes.

Duties in return, under the Fourth Commandment: The Fourth Commandment involves duties on both sides. Those in authority have duties towards those who are entrusted to them. Thus there are:

- duties of parents towards their children;

- duties of teachers towards their pupils;

- duties of employers towards their workers;

- duties of priests towards the members of the Church to whom they minister;

- duties of those in political power towards the citizens of the Country.

The case of employers and workers. The Fourth Commandment applies to relations between employers and workers.

The workers should carry out the work they are paid to do, and not harm their employer. They must not have recourse to violence in defence of their rights. In exchange, employers should have loving care for their workers and give them reasonable wages. They must not impose excessive or dangerous work upon them. Nor must they deflect them from their religious and family duties.

It is *contrary to the love of God* to maintain a spirit of class war. Such an attitude of mind is in total opposition to Jesus's words: "Love one another".

The limits of obedience. Our obedience must never be in opposition to the law of God, as this saying of the Apostles makes clear: "We must obey God rather than men" (Acts 5:29).

QUESTIONS AND ANSWERS TO LEARN

1. What does the Fourth Commandment (Honour your father and your mother) direct us to do?

The Fourth Commandment (Honour your father and your mother) directs:

1. *children* – to love and help their parents, and to obey them;
2. *parents* – to take care of their children;

3. *those who are under authority* – to serve and respect those who have authority over them;

4. *those who are in authority* – to take care of those over whom they have authority.

2. What are the duties of children towards their parents?

Children should obey their parents. They should love their parents, respect them, help them in all their necessities.

3. What are the duties of parents towards their children?

Parents should love their children, by taking care of them, giving them a good religious and moral education, and helping them to find the right direction in life.

4. What are the duties of those under authority towards those who have authority over them?

Those who are under authority should respect those who are in authority over them, and should fulfil all their obligations in the tasks they have undertaken.

5. What are the duties of those in authority towards those under their authority?

Those in authority should take care of those under their authority, and give them everything that has been stipulated in exchange for their work.

6. Does the Fourth Commandment apply to many things?

Yes, the Fourth Commandment applies to many things. It extends to the duties of workers and employers, as it does also to our duties to the Church and to our Country.

7. What are the duties of workers towards their employers?

Workers should:

1. carry out completely and faithfully the work they have undertaken to do,
2. not harm in any way the property of the employer,
3. not do violence to the employer's person,
4. refrain from violence in defence of their rights,
5. never riot against their employer or join with men of disorder.

8. What are the duties of employers towards their workers?

Employers should:

1. have loving care for their workers as brothers and sisters in Christ,
2. give them the wages due to them,
3. not deflect them from their religious and family duties,
4. not make them do harmful work.

9. What are our duties towards the Church?

Our duties towards the Church are: respect, obedience and help.

10. What are our duties towards our Country?

Our duties towards our Country are: obedience to laws that are just; payment of taxes; and service of our Country.

11. Have the Church and our Country any duties towards us?

Yes. The Church and our Country have duties towards us:

1. The bishops and the priests should pass on to us the whole of the teaching received from Jesus Christ.
2. It is up to the Government and Parliament to make laws that are just. The laws they make ought never be opposed to the law of God.

12. Are there limits to obedience?

Yes, obedience has limits. It must never be contrary to the law of God: "We must obey God rather than men".

WORDS TO THINK ABOUT

"We can never be grateful enough for everything a mother has done for us!"

St John Vianney

LESSON 5 – FIFTH COMMANDMENT:

You shall not kill.

WORDS TO READ

God is the Lord and Giver of life, and only He has the right to take it back.

We must not put to death either our neighbour (i.e. any other person) or ourself (suicide). It is likewise forbidden to cause suffering, either physical or mental.

This Commandment forbids everything that could lead to death – jealousy, hate, anger, violence, duelling, and so on.

It is also gravely wrong to lead others into sin through our bad conduct (scandal).

In the Gospel, Jesus requires us to pardon others, and He forbids us to injure our neighbour or to get angry. He declares in the Beatitudes: "Blessed are the meek; the land shall be their inheritance!"

When speaking of the Fifth Commandment one shouldn't forget to refer to all the carelessness by drivers on the roads.

Legitimate defence of persons and of society:

The only cases in which putting someone to death can be allowable are the following:

- *legitimate defence of life:* your own or that of another for whom you are responsible. For example, if you find yourself faced with a would-be murderer who is about to kill you,

- *soldiers* in a *just* war,

- *the death penalty.* In the countries where it exists it should be reserved for the gravest of cases. It is then justified by the principle that authorizes the protecting of society against a dangerous individual.

Finally, human life is sacred *from its very beginning.* It is absolutely forbidden to destroy life, *even in the case of a little being who has just begun to exist* (from conception). One ought never to kill a little unborn baby (abortion), even if that unborn baby is crippled or malformed. Neither ought one to kill an old person who is very ill and incurably so (euthanasia).

QUESTIONS AND ANSWERS TO LEARN

1. What does the Fifth Commandment (You shall not kill) direct us not to do?

The Fifth Commandment (You shall not kill) directs us not to put to death either our neighbour (another person) or ourself (suicide), for God is the Lord and Giver of life, and only He has the right to take it back.

2. What is the extent of the Fifth Commandment?

The Fifth Commandment extends to the whole of human life, from conception onwards. It prohibits the killing of unborn children by abortion, including those crippled or malformed; and it prohibits the killing of old persons who are very ill.

3. What does the Fifth Commandment forbid also?

The Fifth Commandment forbids also:

1. that which can lead to the death of the *body*: anger, jealousy, hate, vengeance, and all forms of violence. Careless driving on the roads also.

2. that (called "scandal") which can lead to the death of the *soul*, to the loss of its supernatural life.

4. What is scandal?

Scandal consists of giving our neighbour, through our words or bad conduct, an occasion of sin.

5. Is scandal a grave sin?

Yes, scandal is a very grave sin, for we are responsible for the evil we have provoked. Jesus said: "Woe to him from whom scandal comes!" (Mt 18:7).

WORDS TO THINK ABOUT

"The way to overthrow the devil when he arouses feelings of hate against those who do us harm is to pray immediately for their conversion."

St John Vianney

LESSON 6 – SIXTH COMMANDMENT:

You shall not commit adultery (nor impurity).

WORDS TO READ

Jesus said: "Blessed are the pure in heart, for they shall see God."

St Paul reminds us that we must respect our body and that of others. "Do you not know that you are the temple of God and that the Spirit of God dwells in you? If anyone destroys the temple of God, him will God destroy. For holy is the temple of God, and this temple you are." (1 Cor 3:16-17).

Purity is therefore a condition for attaining, one day, to the sight of God in heaven – and also for living in the love of God from our time on earth.

God makes Himself known to the soul that is pure. On the other hand, impurity distances us from God.

There is a purity in marriage, from the faithfulness of the husband and wife – that forbids to the husband, and to the wife also, another love outside their home.

For young people, purity is a duty which helps them to prepare for their future. The more pure a young man is, the more will he find a young girl who is worthy of him, and the more will their union stand a chance of being a strong one. It is the same for a girl.

Impurity can bring with it grave health troubles: certain contagious diseases very grave in their consequences of unsound health.

Finally, the mind becomes clouded; one runs the risk of growing used to sin, and of sinking into the worst degradation. One ends up by progressively distancing oneself from prayer and the sacraments to the extent of totally abandoning God!

On the other hand, purity makes one strong, gentle, kind, clear-sighted.

But it is necessary to take steps to guard this treasure of purity. Those steps are many and various:

- avoiding idleness: loving your work and being dedicated to it.

- avoiding over-indulgence in eating and drinking: no excesses of meat or alcoholic drink, no drugs.

- keeping away from bad pals, dangerous surroundings.

- rejecting bad books and bad shows.

- avoiding certain dances and doubtful company.

Purity is *possible with the grace of God.* It is necessary to ask for it by prayer, faithfulness to the Sacrament of Penance, going frequently to communion, and by great devotion to Mary, the Virgin most pure!

QUESTIONS AND ANSWERS TO LEARN

1. What is forbidden by the Sixth Commandment, 'You shall not commit adultery (nor impurity)'?

The Sixth Commandment, You shall not commit adultery (nor impurity), forbids infidelity in marriage, sins of impurity, and everything that can lead to impurity.

2. What are the main causes of impurity?

The main causes of impurity are idleness, over-indulgence in food and drink, bad company, dangerous reading, certain dances and shows, and all sorts of imprudent things.

3. What are the results of impurity?

Impurity can lead to serious health troubles, disorders of mind, hardening in sin, and the sinner's abandonment of God.

4. Can we preserve our purity?

Yes, with the grace of God, we can preserve our purity, through mortification and prudence, through prayer, fidelity to holy communion, and devotion to Mary.

WORDS TO THINK ABOUT

"A pure soul can ask everything of God, even miracles: God will refuse that soul nothing..."

St John Vianney

LESSON 7 – SEVENTH AND EIGHTH COMMANDMENTS:

- **You shall not steal**.
- **You shall not bear false witness**.

WORDS TO READ

We can group together the Seventh and Eighth Commandments. Both of them, indeed, forbid us to injure our neighbour, in regard to his money or belongings or his reputation.

The Seventh Commandment forbids us to steal, whether the theft be of money or of goods. One who has committed a theft, or has omitted to pay what he owes, has an obligation to make restitution.

This Commandment applies to *every question of justice.* That is the case:

1. with the financial aid that we give to the Church and the State;

2. with the duties of employers and workers in their work relations. The employer must pay a just wage, and the worker must do fully the work he or she is employed to do;

3. with contracts and commercial trading, so as to prohibit fraud etc. And those responsible for business enterprises have an obligation to consider the good of persons and not only the increase of profits.

The Eighth Commandment forbids *lying* – that is, telling untruths. But that same Commandment also forbids gossip which discloses something bad about someone to another person who doesn't know it already, *and has no right to know it* – even when what is said is factually true. When it is true, such an attack on someone's reputation is called *detraction*. When what is said is untrue, it is called *calumny*.

All false oaths are forbidden. Disclosing something told to one under the seal of secrecy (e.g. where a professional adviser has been told something in confidence) is also forbidden, unless there is a very grave reason for the disclosure.[1]

In conclusion, one could say that:

- the Seventh Commandment (You shall not steal) completes the Fourth one, for a theft is a lack of respect for the person from whom the theft takes place.
- the Eighth Commandment (You shall not bear false witness) completes the Fifth one, for in a sense calumny destroys someone's life.

QUESTIONS AND ANSWERS TO LEARN

1. What does the Seventh Commandment (You shall not steal) forbid?

The Seventh Commandment (You shall not steal) forbids us to take or wrongly retain the money or goods of others, or to damage such goods through our own fault.

---

1. But no priest, for any reason, is ever allowed to disclose anything told to him in confession (translator).

2. What does the Seventh Commandment extend to?

The Seventh Commandment extends to every question of justice envisaged by the Fourth Commandment – in particular the relations between employers and workers. The employer must pay a just wage, and the worker must supply his or her work in full.

3. What must someone who has broken the Seventh Commandment do?

Someone who has broken the Seventh Commandment must, if he is able, make restitution – that is to say, restore what he has stolen or wrongly retains.

4. What does the Eighth Commandment (You shall not bear false witness) forbid?

The Eighth Commandment (You shall not bear false witness) forbids lying, the making of false oaths, and all words that can harm our neighbour:

- calumny (gossip injurious to reputation, and untrue);
- detraction (gossip injurious to reputation, and true);
- violating a secret, unless for a very grave reason;
- assuming something bad about a person without sufficient foundation (rash judgement).

WORDS TO THINK ABOUT

"In order to receive much, we have to give much!"

St John Vianney

LESSON 8 – NINTH AND TENTH COMMANDMENTS:

You shall not covet your neighbour's wife or your neighbour's goods.

WORDS TO READ

We often bring the Ninth and Tenth Commandments together, because both of them refer to bad desires, which are consented to.

Indeed a bad desire to which one consents, and harbours in one's mind, is the continual occasion of a fall. As has been well written: "To desire what is evil is itself evil. Impure thoughts corrupt our minds and can lead to immoral actions."

The Ninth Commandment forbids, not only desiring another man's wife, but also all impure thoughts which can lead to sin. By this short form of words, we must understand that someone who is not married ought not to desire a woman who is already joined in marriage, and he ought not to desire an unmarried girl except with the intention of marrying her.

As for one who is married: he ought not to desire any woman or young girl other than his wife.

It is the same for a woman with regard to men; she ought not to harbour any desire outside marriage.

The Ninth Commandment, like the Sixth (already studied) places great value on the Sacrament of Marriage and forbids everything that holds this Sacrament in contempt. Further, both those Commandments call for preservation of the treasure of purity. They are opposed to the loosening of standards that some would like to introduce into morals, and which is the cause of widespread immorality in the world.

The Tenth Commandment also refers to desires – not for persons, though, but for *goods* – for objects which belong to others. Such desires, if one harbours them, can lead to theft in all its forms.

QUESTIONS AND ANSWERS TO LEARN

1. What does the Ninth Commandment (You shall not covet your neighbour's wife) forbid?

The Ninth Commandment (You shall not covet your neighbour's wife) forbids sins of desire, harboured and consented to, which can lead to impurity or to adultery.

2. What does the Tenth Commandment (You shall not covet your neighbour's goods) forbid?

The Tenth Commandment (You shall not covet your neighbour's goods) forbids unjust desires for what belongs to our neighbour.

3. Why is harbouring bad desires forbidden?

It is forbidden since it is wrong in itself and they are a near (not remote) occasion of sin.

WORDS TO THINK ABOUT

"If we wish to preserve purity of soul and of body, we must mortify our imagination."

St John Vianney

LESSON 9 – COMMANDMENTS OF THE CHURCH

WORDS TO READ

The commandments of the Church are precise requirements laid down by the Church to help Catholics fulfil the duties of our religion ("religion" meaning what binds one lovingly to Almighty God). These requirements have reference to prayer, the Sacraments, and a spirit of penitence.

The first commandment of the Church is supplementary to the Third Commandment of God: the keeping of Sunday holy, through Mass attendance especially.

To Sundays are to be added the Holy Days of Obligation designated by the Church in each country. In England and Wales, these are: Christmas Day, Saints Peter and Paul, the Assumption of the Blessed Virgin Mary, and All Saints' Day.

Other commandments of the Church lay down that we must go to confession and receive holy communion at least once a year! We should have at heart to do much better than that.

Further commandments of the Church remind us of the need for penance and mortification. This reminder takes the form of Catholics being obligated, on certain days (according as the Church has specified for those days) to "*fast*" (eat smaller meals) and/or to "*abstain*" (do without meat – meat being a symbol of food that is too rich, too abundant). This penance is called for in union with Jesus' fasting in the desert.

QUESTIONS AND ANSWERS TO LEARN

1. To be saved, is it enough to obey the Commandments of God?

To be saved, we Catholics must also obey the commandments of the Church.

2. What are the commandments of the Church?

The commandments of the Church are:

1. To attend Mass on Sundays and Holy Days of Obligation, and to refrain work and activities which could impede keeping those days holy.

2. To go to confession at least once a year.

3. Humbly to receive the Blessed Sacrament at least once a year, during the Easter season.

4. To abstain from meat on the days designated by the Church. In England and Wales, those who are 14 and over are required to abstain from meat on Ash Wednesday and Good Friday, and (from 16th September 2011)[1] *on all other Fridays,* except those on which a solemn feastday falls.

5. To fast (i.e to eat considerably less than normal) on the days designated by the Church. In England and Wales, adults (i.e. those who are 18 and over) are required, until the beginning of their sixtieth year, to fast on Ash Wednesday and Good Friday.

6. To contribute to the material support of our clergy, according to our ability.

---

1. Restoration, by the Catholic Bishops' Conference of England and Wales, May 2011, of former specific obligation and practice.

3. What do the commandments of the Church about Mass attendance direct us to do?

The commandments of the Church about Mass attendance require us to be present at Mass on each Sunday (or the Vigil Mass on Saturday evening), and also on each Holy Day of Obligation (or the Vigil Mass for that day, on the previous evening), unless there is a serious reason to the contrary such as illness.

In England and Wales, the Holy Days of Obligation are: Christmas Day, Saints Peter and Paul, the Assumption of the Blessed Virgin Mary, and All Saints' Day.

4. What does the commandment of the Church about confession direct us to do?

The commandment of the Church about confession requires us to receive the Sacrament of Penance at least once a year.

5. What does the commandment of the Church about going to communion direct us to do?

The commandment of the Church about going to communion requires us to receive the Blessed Sacrament at least once a year, during the Easter season.

6. What does the commandment of the Church about abstaining from meat direct us to do?

The commandment of the Church about abstaining from meat requires us, if we are 14 or over, not to eat meat on Ash Wednesday and Good Friday, and (see page 130) *on all other Fridays*, except Fridays on which a solemnity falls.

7. What does the commandment of the Church about fasting require us to do? Do you fast when you become an adult?

The commandment of the Church about fasting requires that adults (i.e. those 18 and over), who have not reached their sixtieth year, shall fast (eat considerably less than normal) on Ash Wednesday and Good Friday.

WORDS TO THINK ABOUT

"Some people find religion tiresome, but that is because they do not have the Holy Spirit!"

St John Vianney

LESSON 10 – SIN

WORDS TO READ

Pride hurled the rebel angels down into hell.

Pride is the source of sin.

The first sin, that of Adam and Eve, *original sin,* was an act of pride: "You will become like gods," the devil had said to them.

Every sin is *an act of pride,* a refusal to submit to God.

We have been created with *free will.* Because of this freedom, our will can accept good, or (alas!) refuse it.

Every sin is a disobedience, but the gravity of it can vary. We distinguish between:

1. *Mortal sin:* when there is grave matter, with full consent and a clear idea of its gravity. Such a sin, a mortal sin, makes us lose the state of grace.

2. *Venial sin:* when there is not grave matter, or where the person gives only incomplete consent, or does not know the grave nature of the sinful act or omission. Venial sins do not destroy the state of grace, but they weaken our soul.

One may say that the different sins can be brought down to seven principal types. These, called "capital sins" (or, if habitual, "deadly vices") are:

– *pride:* attributing to oneself the glory that belongs only to God.

- *avarice:* loving our possessions and keeping them to ourselves, ignoring the needs of others.

- *envy:* wanting to have what belongs to others. One can be jealous of their beauty, their health, their success, their riches.

- *wrath:* strong anger. One flares up, loses control of oneself, returns evil for evil.

- *lust:* loving bad pleasures, things which purity forbids.

- *gluttony:* eating and drinking to excess, thus risking harm to one's health.

- *sloth:* laziness. Not being bothered to work, neglecting the duties of one's state of life, falling into idleness.

These sins are called "capital" sins because they are at the origin of all the other sins.

QUESTIONS AND ANSWERS TO LEARN

1. What is sin?

Sin is a refusal given to God and to what He requires of us.

2. How many kinds of sin are there?

There are two kinds of sin, mortal and venial.

3. What is mortal sin?

Mortal sin is a disobedience of God –

    1. in a grave matter,
    2. with full consent, and

3. with a clear idea of the gravity of the sinful act or omission.

4. What is venial sin?
Venial sin is a disobedience of God in a matter which is not grave, or with only part consent, or committed by one who does not know the gravity of the sinful act or omission.

5. What is the effect of mortal sin?
A mortal sin deprives the soul of sanctifying grace and (unless repented of and forgiven) destines it to the eternal death of hell.

6. What is the effect of venial sin?
Venial sin lessens our fervour and makes us weaker when temptation comes.

7. What can all sins be brought down to?
Sins can be brought down to seven, which are called the *capital* sins.

8. What are the seven capital sins?
The seven capital sins are: pride, avarice, envy, wrath (strong anger), lust, gluttony and sloth (laziness).

9. What is meant by "capital sins"?
"Capital sins" means the principal sins, because those sins are the origin and root of all the other sins.

LESSON 11 – THE VIRTUES

WORDS TO READ

Virtues are the lasting dispositions of our soul which point us in the direction of God and help us to be good.

We distinguish between the theological virtues and the moral virtues.

The *theological* virtues are those that have God as their immediate object; they point us in the direction of Him. These theological virtues are:

– *Faith,* by which we believe everything which the Father has revealed through His Son Jesus Christ, and which the Church teaches us.

– *Hope,* by which we desire God as our Supreme Good and look forward to receiving everything that has been promised us: His grace in our life upon earth, and the happiness of Life Eternal in heaven.

– *Charity (love),* by which we love God above all else, and love our neighbour as ourself for love of God.

Those three *theological* virtues are necessary for our salvation. The *moral* virtues are those that help us to be good; they guide our conduct.

Among the moral virtues, we give the name "cardinal virtues" to some of them. "Cardinal" comes from a Latin word meaning "hinge", like the hinge on a door. Calling certain virtues "cardinal" signifies that other moral virtues hinge on them, are based upon them.

The cardinal moral virtues are:

– *prudence,* which directs our actions and makes us choose and employ means that are good.

– *justice* (righteousness), which makes us give to each person what is due to him or her.

– *fortitude,* which makes us confront difficulties and dangers (even death) in order to serve God and our neighbour.

– *temperance,* which helps us to restrain our passions (strong emotions) and desires, especially the pleasures of the senses, and to moderate the use of even good things that gratify our senses.

Other moral virtues. We can think of each of the seven capital sins as having its own opposite moral virtue:

– the opposite of pride: the virtue of *humility*;

– the opposite of avarice: the virtue of *liberality* (generosity in giving to others);

– the opposite of envy: the virtue of *fraternal love*;

– the opposite of wrath: the virtue of *meekness*;

– the opposite of lust: the virtue of *chastity*;

– the opposite of gluttony: the virtue of *temperance*;

– the opposite of sloth: the virtue of *diligence.*

Our Lord Jesus Christ commended practice of the virtues when, in the Sermon on the Mount, He taught the *Beatitudes* ("Blessed are..."). "Beatitude" comes from a Latin word that means "happy" or "blessed". These Beatitudes, eight in number, are listed in answer number 16 below.

QUESTIONS AND ANSWERS TO LEARN

1. What is a virtue?

A virtue is a good habit, a lasting disposition which inclines us to being good and avoiding evil.

2. How many kinds of virtue are there?

There are two kinds of virtue: theological virtues and moral virtues.

3. What is a theological virtue?

A theological virtue is a virtue that has as its immediate object God, considered as our super-natural end, and which points us towards Him.

4. Which are the theological virtues?

The theological virtues are faith, hope and charity.

5. Are the theological virtues necessary for our salvation?

Yes, the theological virtues are necessary for our salvation, for they point our mind and our will to God.

6. What is faith?

Faith is a super-natural virtue by which we firmly believe all that God has revealed.

7. What is hope?

Hope is a super-natural virtue by which we desire God and await with confidence all that He has promised.

8. What is charity?

Charity is a super-natural virtue by which we love God more than all else because He is infinitely good, and love our neighbour as ourself for love of God.

9. Make an act of faith.

"O my God, I firmly believe all the truths which you have revealed and which your Church teaches, because you are Truth itself and can neither deceive nor be deceived."

10. Make an act of hope.

"O my God, I hope with a firm confidence that you will give me, through the merits of Jesus Christ, grace in this world and, if I obey your Commandments, eternal happiness in heaven, because you have promised this and you always keep your promises."

11. Make an act of charity.

"O my God, I love you with my whole heart and above all else, because you are so good and so kind; and I love my neighbour as myself for love of you."

12. What is a moral virtue?

A moral virtue is a virtue that has as its immediate object good actions, in accord with right reason.

13. What are the principal moral virtues?

The principal moral virtues are prudence, justice, fortitude and temperance. These are called cardinal virtues. The word "cardinal" comes from the Latin for "hinge", and these cardinal virtues are ones on which all morality hinges.

14. What are the moral virtues that are the opposites of the seven capital sins?

The moral virtues that are the opposites of the seven capital sins are: humility, liberality (i.e. generosity in giving to others), fraternal love, meekness, chastity, temperance and diligence.

15. Jesus commended certain moral virtues to us when He declared "blessed" those who practise them.

Yes. He did so in what are called the Beatitudes.

16. What are these eight Beatitudes?

The following are the eight Beatitudes:

"Blessed are the poor in spirit;
  the Kingdom of Heaven is theirs.

"Blessed are the meek;
  the land shall be their inheritance.

"Blessed are those who mourn;
  they shall be comforted.

"Blessed are those who hunger and thirst for
  righteousness; they shall be satisfied.

"Blessed are the merciful;
   they shall obtain mercy.

"Blessed are the pure in heart;
  they shall see God.

"Blessed are the peacemakers;
  they shall be called children of God.

"Blessed are those who suffer persecution for
  the sake of righteousness; the Kingdom of
  Heaven is theirs."

LESSON 12 – PRAYER

WORDS TO READ

We can reach God – *by prayer!*

Prayer is often defined as "the raising of our mind and heart to God".

In prayer, we can adore, give thanks, ask for forgiveness, obtain graces for ourselves and for others.

A distinction to be made is that between a *spirit* of prayer and the *times* of prayer.

A *spirit of prayer* consists of staying always in union with God in the midst of all our activities, like a little child holding on to the hand of its dad or mum.

The *times of prayer* are those parts of the day which we reserve for God, to speak to God, to talk with Him.

How do we pray?

1. *By thought* (mental prayer). We remain silent, we are speaking inside of us.

A French saint (St Charles de Foucauld) used to say: "Praying is thinking of God while loving Him."

2. *By words* (vocal prayer). We can utter words, say set prayers like the Our Father and the Hail Mary.

We can make invocations in the way that one Cistercian monk used to. He would repeat softly (even at night, when he awoke): "O you who love me so much, may I love you, O Lord!"

Private prayer and public prayer

Private prayer is that which we pray in quiet, by ourself in the presence of God. It is good also to pray together as a family, morning and evening.

Public prayer is where a parish, or a group, are assembled together for prayer such as liturgical prayer (Holy Mass and Divine Office) or the public recitation of the Rosary in honour of Our Lady.

Jesus commended to us both kinds of prayer. He said: "When you pray, go into your room and close the door, and pray to your Father in secret."

He also said: "Where two or three are gathered together in my name, there am I in the midst of them."

In order to be saved, prayer is absolutely necessary for us. Let us remember Jesus's instruction: "Watch and pray!"

QUESTIONS AND ANSWERS TO LEARN

1. What is prayer?

Prayer is the raising of our mind and heart to God, to adore Him, to thank Him, to request forgiveness, and to obtain graces for ourself and for others.

2. Is it necessary for us to pray?

Yes, it is necessary for us to pray, for it is the will of God that we do so.

3. How can we pray?

We can pray:

1. by thought: that is mental prayer;
2. by words: that is vocal prayer.

4. How many kinds of vocal prayer are there?

There are two kinds of vocal prayer:

1. private prayer, alone or as a family;
2. public prayer, organised in churches.

5. What are the principal prayers?

The principal prayers are:

–   The Our Father (or Pater Noster), which is addressed to God the Father.
–   The Hail Mary (or Ave Maria), which is addressed to the Blessed Virgin.

WORDS TO THINK ABOUT

"How happy we are when we pray!... A little creature like us, talking to God who is so great and so powerful!"

St John Vianney

Some references to other concise publications

(The pages and paragraphs given are not exclusive, but may be particularly useful.)
Generally, please see Translator's Note on page 155.

Key:

P/Ctm *A Catechism of Christian Doctrine* (the original "Penny Catechism"), pub. Catholic Truth Society, £1.95.

H/P *Credo: The Catholic Faith Explained,* by Fr Marcus Holden and Fr Andrew Pinsent, pub. Catholic Truth Society, £2.95.

Cpend *Compendium of the Catechism of the Catholic Church,* pub. Catholic Truth Society, £6.95.

BOOK ONE: Our Credo, Truths to Believe

Lesson 1 – God.
   God: P/Ctm, paras. 17-25; Cpend, para. 39.
   We and God: P/Ctm, paras. 1-2; H/P, page 9; Cpend, paras. 2-4.

Lesson 2 – The Mystery of the Holy Trinity.
   P/Ctm, paras. 24-28; H/P, pp. 31-33; Cpend, para. 45.

Lesson 3 – The Creation and the Angels.
   Creation: P/Ctm, para. 19; Cpend, para. 59.
   Angels: Cpend, paras. 60-61.

Lesson 4 – The Creation of Man.
   P/Ctm, paras. 1-6; H/P, pp. 11-12 ("What is special..."); Cpend, paras. 66, 70.

Lesson 5 – *Original Sin. Incarnation and Redemption:*
The Fall of Man, and Original Sin: P/Ctm, paras.
114-119; H/P, pp. 12-13; Cpend, paras. 75-77
(also full CCC, para. 390).
The Redeemer foretold: H/P, p. 13 (last question);
Cpend, paras. 78, 102, 21.

Lesson 6 – *The Mystery of the Incarnation.*
Jesus Christ. P/Ctm, paras. 31-45; H/P, pp. 19-21;
Cpend, paras. 86-87, 80.

Lesson 7 – *The Blessed Virgin Mary.*
P/Ctm, paras. 47-51, 160-168b; H/P, pp. 43-44;
Cpend, paras. 94-100.

Lesson 8 – *The Childhood of Jesus.*
Word-pictures of the first Christmas:
Birth of Jesus and adoration by shepherds:
Luke 2:1-20.
Visit and adoration by the Three Wise Men:
Matthew 2:1-12.
Wording of Christmas Carols (usefully illustrative,
whatever the season).
Flight into Egypt: Matthew 2:13-23.
Jesus's hidden life: Cpend, para. 104.

Lesson 9 – *The Public Life of Jesus. Teaching. Miracles.*
H/P, pp. 24-25; Cpend, paras. 107-111.

Lesson 10 – *The Mystery of the Redemption: Death
of Jesus Christ:*
*Christ our Saviour, God-Man, has reconciled man
with God:* P/Ctm, paras. 52-61; H/P, pp. 27-28;
Cpend, paras. 119-123.
His descent into "Hell" ("Limbo"): P/Ctm, paras.
63-65; H/P, p. 28; Cpend, para. 125.

Lesson 11 – *The Mystery of the Redemption: Resurrection and Ascension.*
P/Ctm, paras. 66-70; H/P, p. 29; Cpend, paras. 126-127, 132.

Lesson 12 – *The Holy Spirit.*
P/Ctm, paras. 77-82 ; Cpend, paras. 136-140.

Lesson 13 – *The Church.*
The Church: P/Ctm, paras. 84-101; H/P, pp. 35-36; Cpend, paras. 182-183, 172-173. (See also page 52, n., of the present book.)
Her transmission of Revelation (Scripture and Tradition): H/P, pp. 39-40; Cpend, paras. 11-14, 16-17.

Lesson 14 – *The Members of the Church (Communion of Saints).*
P/Ctm, paras. 102-109; H/P, pp. 36-37; Cpend, paras. 195, 210-211. ("The Communion of Saints" is more than the Church in heaven, as H/P, p. 37 might be read as saying. It consists of holy persons in the Church on earth, in purgatory and in heaven.)

Lessons 15 – *The Forgiveness of Sins.*
This is material that will be developed in later Lessons in Book Two, on the Sacraments of Penance and also Baptism, and in Book Three, on Sin. But good preparation at this stage in: P/Ctm, paras. 110-113, 119-127; H/P, pp. 68-69; Cpend, paras. 200-201; 171.

Lesson 16 – *The Resurrection of the Body and Last Judgement. Life Eternal.*
– *After death, our existence continues for ever, eternally:* P/Ctm, paras. 5-6 (soul); Cpend, paras.

205, 203 (body also, after the Resurrection of the Body).

- *Particular judgement, at moment of our individual death (determining our final destination for eternity – Heaven or Hell):* P/Ctm, paras. 76, 332; H/P, p. 44; Cpend, para. 208 (its word "retribution" includes glorious reward).

- *Resurrection of the Body, and the Last Judgement of everyone at the end of the world:* P/Ctm, paras 71-75; H/P, pp. 44-45; Cpend, paras. 214-215.

- *Mary already taken up, body as well as soul, into Heaven:* P/Ctm, paras. 168a-168b; H/P, p. 44 ("What is her Assumption?").

- *Life Eternal, in the sense of everlasting happiness with God in Heaven:* P/Ctm, paras. 130-133; H/P, p. 45; Cpend, para. 209.

- *Purgatory:* P/Ctm, paras. 106-109; H/P, p. 45; Cpend, paras. 210-211.

- *Hell:* P/Ctm, para. 125; H/P, p. 45; Cpend, paras. 212-213.

Lesson 17 – The Credo, or Apostles' Creed. P/Ctm, paras. 13-15.

BOOK TWO: Grace and the Sacraments

Lesson 1 – Grace. H/P, p. 75; Cpend, paras. 422-426.

Lesson 2 – The Sacraments. P/Ctm, paras. 249-255; H/P, pp. 48-49; Cpend, paras. 224, 231.

Lesson 3 – *Baptism.*
P/Ctm, paras. 256-259; H/P, pp. 51-52 ; Cpend, paras. 261-262 (see also full CCC, paras. 1257-1261); Cpend, para. 264 (name at baptism).

Lesson 4 – *Confirmation.*
P/Ctm, paras. 262-265; H/P, pp. 52-53; Cpend, para. 268.

Lesson 5 – *The Holy Eucharist (Blessed Sacrament).*
P/Ctm, paras. 266-268; H/P, pp. 56-57 (as Presence); Cpend, paras. 282-283, 286.

Lesson 6 – *The Sacrifice of the Mass.*
P/Ctm, paras. 274-280; H/P, pp. 55-56 (as Sacrifice); Cpend, paras. 272-273, 280, 289.

Lesson 7 – *Holy Communion.*
P/Ctm, paras. 270-272; H/P, p. 57 (as Food for our soul); Cpend, para. 292, 294. Also full CCC, paras. 1391-1395, 1402.

Lesson 8 – *The Sacrament of Penance, or of Reconciliation.*
P/Ctm, paras. 281-286; H/P, p. 59; Cpend, paras. 297-298, 302, 304, 306-307, 309.

Lesson 9 – *Contrition.*
P/Ctm, paras. 287-294; H/P, p. 60; Cpend, para. 300.

Lesson 10 – *Confession and Satisfaction (Penance repairing damage of sin):*
Confession: P/Ctm, paras. 295-297; H/P, pp. 59-60, 99-101; Cpend, paras. 304, 306, 309.
Satisfaction: P/Ctm, paras. 298-299; H/P, p. 60
Indulgences: P/Ctm, para. 300; Cpend, para. 312.

Lesson 11 – *Anointing of the Sick.*
P/Ctm, paras. 301-304; H/P, p. 61; Cpend, paras.

315-317, 319; 320 (Blessed Sacrament as Viaticum).

Lesson 12 – Holy Orders.
P/Ctm, para. 305; H/P, pp. 64-65; Cpend, paras. 322, 331-333.

Lesson 13 – *Marriage.*
P/Ctm, paras. 306-312; H/P, pp. 63-64; Cpend, paras. 337-339, 342-343.
Separation: Cpend, para. 348.
Divorce and Annulment: ("Annulment", more precisely "Declaration of Nullity") H/P, p. 64.

Additional Note – Important

Rome's fine document of guidance (available online), *The Truth and Meaning of Human Sexuality,* affirms that it is parents (not schools, much less the State) who, knowing them as individuals as they do, have the primary right to give sexual information to their children in the way they deem best for them, and in addition have a responsibility for the formation of their children in the acceptance of authentic morality. Firmly rejecting the notion of giving unnecessary sex information to **very young children**, those in "the years of innocence" ("premature", and the violation of innocence endangers the "spiritual, moral and emotional development" of children so young: paras. 78-84), the document also appears to envisage that some Catholic parents – in supplementation of parental efforts or otherwise – will expect and wish their children at Catholic **secondary** schools to receive there some guidance on sexual morality, fully conforming to the teaching of the Church.

In whatever role this is given, in Lesson 13 or

a separate context of sex education and morality, the Church's teaching (a) that sexual relations are morally permissible *only within marriage* (which means between a man and a woman) and not outside or before marriage (full CCC, para. 2390), and (b) that artificial contraception is morally impermissible as being not "open to the transmission of life" (full CCC, para. 2366), are amongst the matters to be taught – delicately and without unnecessary detail, yet firmly and supportively of the Catholic teaching – at an appropriate secondary school age.

Parents are entitled to assurance on all the above.

BOOK THREE: The Moral Law.
The Commandments.

Lesson 1- *The Ten Commandments of God.*
    Cpend, paras. 434-435, 440-441; HP, p. 73;
    P/Ctm, paras. 334-343, 348-354.

Lesson 2 – *First Commandment (You shall worship God, and God only).*
    Cpend, para. 443; P/Ctm, paras. 182, 186-187.

Lesson 3 – *Second Commandment (You shall not take the name of God in vain). Third Commandment (Remember to keep Sunday holy):*
    Second Commandment: P/Ctm, paras. 189-190 (avoidance of using the name of God irreverently or lightly); Cpend, paras. 447-448.
    Third Commandment: Cpend, para. 453.

Lesson 4 – *Fourth Commandment (You shall honour your father and your mother).*
    P/Ctm, paras. 197-203; Cpend, paras. 459-462, 464-465.

Lesson 5 – *Fifth Commandment (You shall not kill).*
P/Ctm, paras. 206-208; Cpend, paras. 466-467, 470-472; also 469 (capital punishment, rarely if ever justified); 483-486 (war); 473 (scandal).

Lesson 6 – *Sixth Commandment (You shall not commit adultery (nor impurity).*
P/Ctm, paras. 210-213; Cpend, para. 493. See also Additional Note on pages 151-152 above (sexual matters, and promotion of chastity and purity).

Lesson 7 – *Seventh Commandment (You shall not steal). Eighth Commandment (You shall not bear false witness):*
Seventh Commandment: P/Ctm, paras. 215-216.
Eighth Commandment: P/Ctm, paras. 220-222; Cpend, para. 524.

Lesson 8 – *Ninth Commandment (You shall not covet your neighbour's wife). Tenth Commandment (You shall not covet your neighbour's goods):*
Ninth Commandment: Cpend, paras. 528-529.
Tenth Commandment: P/Ctm, para. 227; Cpend, para. 531.

Lesson 9 – *Commandments of the Church. (There are slight differences in the arrangement and numbering of these Church "precepts", i.e. Commandments.)* H/P, p. 82; Cpend, para. 432; P/Ctm, paras. 228, 232.

Lesson 10 – *Sin.*
Sin: Cpend, paras. 391-398; H/P, pp. 68-69.
The *seven capital sins (or deadly vices):* P/Ctm, paras. 324-325; H/P, pp. 80-81.
Responsibility for sins of others: Cpend, para. 399; P/Ctm, paras. 328-329.

Lesson 11 – *The Virtues.*

- *Virtues:* H/P, pp. 79-80; Cpend, para. 377.

- *Theological virtues (Faith, Hope and Charity):*
  P/Ctm, paras. 8, 313-314 (theological virtues);
  9-12 (faith); 135-137 and 179 (hope); 169-171
  (charity); **H/P**, p.79; **Cpend**, paras. 384-385
  (theological virtues); 386, 27, 29 (faith);
  387 (hope); 388 (charity). For "Charity",
  see also "Commandments" and "Grace".

- *Cardinal moral virtues:*
  P/Ctm, paras. 316-317; H/P, pp. 79-80.

- *Moral virtues which are the opposites of the seven
  capital sins:* P/Ctm, para. 324; H/P, p. 81.

  Terminology: Moral virtues are sometimes
  called "human" or "natural" virtues.

- *Beatitudes:* H/P, pp. 76-77.

Lesson 12 – *Prayer.*

- *Prayer, and personal Christian life:* P/Ctm, paras.
  141-142; H/P, pp. 83-84, 87-89; Cpend, paras.
  569-575.

- *The "Our Father" and other important prayers:*
  P/Ctm, paras. 144-157, pages 82-88; H/P,
  pp. 91-93; Cpend, paras. 578, 587.

- *Praying the Mass:* H/P, pp. 95-97.

- *Prayers to Our Lady, Saints and Angels:* P/Ctm.
  paras. 158-165.

- *Catholic Devotions:* H/P, pp. 103-105.

- See also P/Ctm, 355-370 (Daily Exercise).

- *Four Last Things:* P/Ctm, para. 332.

TRANSLATOR'S NOTE
(including practical points about the book)

I consider this book – by the late Hugues d'Orfeuille, an experienced and sound French catechist – to be a remarkable and most important framework, perceptively worded.

I have sought to follow the French wording very closely in translating, save where I felt that mis-understanding might be caused by doing so or that a limited expansion would shed further light, or where the French text would be inapplicable to circumstances in England and Wales. In once case I have replaced a long analogy by a direct explanation.

Teachers will note the author's comment that the "Questions and answers to learn" *should first of all be clearly explained to pupils.* What supplementary material might be helpful for this?

Feeling that *concise* material would be the most useful in the hands of teachers (not to speak of pupils too), I have given cross-references on pages 146-154. They include references to the Catechism of the Catholic Church (CCC) – or, more precisely, to its *Compendium.* (The Compendium, in turn, gives paragraph references to the full CCC, which can be consulted for further guidance.) Neither of these had appeared when M. d'Orfeuille's little jewel of a work was published in 1983. (CCC guided my translation where this was required.)

I have also given cross-references to two other concise publications – both of them, like the Compendium, published by the Catholic Truth Society. Both are inexpensive and excellent, and they complement each other.

Some of the cross-reference numbers are repeated, overlapping as between Lessons.

All the Lessons in the present work are important, but not all of them contain same amount of material. So packed with very important points are some of the Lessons, that for a deep coverage of their particular subject they will require a much greater time allocation than for other Lessons.

Learning

The warmth with which both the author and Dr. Huant in the Introduction commend the practice of learning by heart will be remarked also. This has an honourable tradition behind it; and in *Catechesi Tradendae* (1979) Pope John Paul II wrote: "...should we not attempt to put [the human faculty of memory] back into use in an intelligent and even an original way in catechesis...?" He added: "A certain memorization of the words of Jesus, of important Bible passages, of the Ten Commandments, of the formulas of profession of the faith, of the liturgical texts, of the essential prayers, of key doctrinal ideas, etc. ... is a real need... The blossoms, if we may call them that, of faith and piety do not grow in the desert places of a memory-less catechesis." However, he stressed that what is memorized must be "properly understood"; it must "be taken in and gradually understood in depth..." (55).

It is true that some of the answers set out in the present work are rather long, and this should be taken into account. But I think the author's precision and clarity will be of great service to both teachers and pupils even in classes where pupils are not required to memorize, or where they are so required simply in the case of particularly important formulations.

Mysteries

Along with all the precision comes, rightly, a repeated use of the phrase "The Mystery of..." The author, on page 25, gives an excellent definition of "Mystery" in this sense: "A Mystery is a Truth that we ought to believe, but that we cannot fully understand because it goes beyond what our minds can grasp." For the human mind remains finite, and God is Infinite. Frank Sheed wrote: "A Mystery is not something that we can know nothing about: it is only something that the mind cannot *wholly* know." "It is," he said, "to be thought of ... as a gallery into which we can progress deeper and deeper, though we can never reach the end – yet every step of our progress is immeasurably satisfying."

"He", "Him" and "His"

When we use these pronouns to refer to God, the context may show that we are referring to the Father or to one of the other Persons of the Holy Trinity. But sometimes we use these pronouns, "He", "Him" and "His", to refer simply to "God" – and God *is* the Trinity, the Three-in-One! If this puzzles us, we have to remember that our human language is altogether inadequate when speaking of the Mystery of the Trinity. However, it is the only language we have.

Title

When the French original of this work was first published in 1983, it was under the title *Catéchisme avec le Curé d'Ars.* I have adopted the title of a later edition, *Catéchisme avec pensées du Curé d'Ars,* thinking it more descriptively apt.

The "Swiss cardinal" mentioned on page 78 was

Cardinal Journet. The "Cistercian monk" mentioned on pages 107and 143 was Dom Chautard.

Acknowledgements

It is a joy to have the Preface from Bishop Patrick O'Donoghue, and I wish to express my gratitude to him here.

I thank especially Fr Ian G. Kelly for his advancing of this book upon its way. I am immensely grateful also to Fr Anthony Kay, Vicar General of the Salford Diocese, and Fr Ian Farrell of that Diocese, for their kindness and patient help. I thank Fr Aidan Nichols OP for his helpful advice on two points of wording I raised with him.

I wish also to express gratitude to Fr Joseph Eruppakkatt SSP of ST PAULS Publishing, Mr Stephen Moseling of ST PAULS Bookshop, London; and to Mr James Crowley, of Manchester, without whose expert IT assistance I would have stumbled in that field even more than I did.

I saw and bought copies of the French original, years ago, at the Miraculous Medal Chapel in the Rue du Bac. I hope Our Lady's blessing and her intercessions – together with those of St John Vianney – will accompany its translation.

Alan Bancroft